MW00901690

Supply Chain

Handbook for 3PL, Consultants

and Sales Executives

A must have for 3PL's, freight forwarders, steam ship lines, airlines, consultants and anyone that sells and promotes services that impact the supply chain, globally or nationally.

- and –

What a customer of Supply Chain Services can expect or demand from a supply chain provider.

Ralph Malmros

ISBN-13:

978-1463723651

ISBN-10:

1463723652

DEDICATION

I want to dedicate this book to every Supply Chain professional that believes in continuous improvement of everything we do in our industry.

- and -

To share ideas and thoughts that will promote an elevation of collaboration and efficiency with our customers.

To create a better understanding of the <u>total</u> Supply Chain, and help professionals become even more successful.

- and -

To my wife for her love and understanding and who has supported my efforts over the years.

About the Author

Ralph Malmros is a Global Operations Supply Chain and Logistics expert including B2C and B2B operations, fulfillment, IT systems and business process strategy. He has worldwide experience in design and implementation of:

SUPPLY CHAINS	**OPERATIONS**	**ECOMMERCE**
WAREHOUSING	**DISTRIBUTION**	**ASSEMBLY**
STRATEGY	**CALL CENTERS**	**PEAK SHIPPING**
IT - SOFTWARE	**DELIVERY MODELS**	**SITE LOCATION**

He has a comprehensive understanding of end to end supply chain and ecommerce business enterprise. Including imported product and raw material, through manufacturing, merchandising, marketing, fulfillment, distribution, customer service, call centers, delivery carriers and the system requirements to support total operations.

He gives seminars, provides training and consulting advice for Supply Chain, Ecommerce, Start-Ups, Importing, Exporting and Manufacturing organizations. He can be reached at 949-278- 9669 or via email at Ralph@montclairconsultants.com.

Supply Chain

Handbook for 3PL, Consultants

and Sales Executives

Practical information you can read daily and apply immediately.

To become excellent in any area of Supply Chain Sales you have to understand the total Supply Chain.

Table of contents

INTRODUCTION

The difference between Supply Chain and Logistics

Part One – The Start in Sales

Research and preparation for sales

Reporting formats for Supply Chain executives

Part Two – The Next Level

- **Sales Management – National and Global**

Rejection, is it personal?

How to sell to the Manufacturer-CPG

Part Three – Supply Chain sales for Ocean freight, Truck, Warehousing, Distribution, Air Freight and Parcel

- **How to sell without lowering the rate**

- **Selling Value over Price**

INTRODUCTION

The Supply Chain represents a more important part of our daily lives then we realize. Most of what we do today in manufacturing, retail, ecommerce or services is in one way or another dependent on supply chains. Not having proper training and a clear understanding of the total supply chain will negatively impact our services.

I have written this book to improve the collaboration between the supply chain sales professionals and the customers of supply chain services. It is designed to point out opportunities for a sales executive to encourage the collaborate process that is required to promote successful supply chain services.

The importance of understanding the total supply chain and being able to provide adequate services to any segment in the supply chain, at any given time is paramount.

The aspiration is for the sales professional to gain a better insight to the sales target and their requirements within the supply chain. The thought is to share both sides of the sales process thus creating a better acceptance and understanding of the sales promise and the compliance of operational requirements.

One of the most important parts of supply chain management is the visibility within the supply chain. The difficulty in obtaining better visibility lies within a true collaborative process across all vendors, participants and system integration.

For this purpose several different levels in sales from entry level to management have been addressed. It is designed to create insight and understanding at all levels of the sales process.

Frankly too much time is wasted within the actual sales procedure. Time, energy and expense can be saved if you have a better understanding of the sales practice.

I have accumulated some ideas, helpful points and techniques that can assist all of us in reducing the time it takes to close the sale.

I would be exceptionally pleased if the interactive scenarios I discuss from the various segments of the supply chain can provide a better understanding and insight to the overall supply chain.

Nothing happens in business before someone has made a sale!

I TOUCH THE FUTURE, I TEACH

-Anonymous-

The difference between Supply Chain and Logistics ! ?

Throughout this book I use the term Supply Chain and Logistics very freely and in an interactive way. I have collected some points of view from a variety of Supply Chain/Logistics Professionals just to get an idea of what our professionals really think this is.

These are all good points but, if you are confused after reading these comments, please make up your own mind as to what it represents to you. The important issue at hand is like Nike says it with their trademark slogan "Just do it".

What ever this Logistics is I want some of it!!

Admiral McGregor, Pacific Fleet WWII

Here are the comments from "our" professionals:

"Logistics is the management of the flow of goods and services between the point of origin and the point of consumption in order to meet the requirements of customers. Logistics involves the integration of information, transportation, inventory, warehousing, material handling, and packaging, and occasionally security. Logistics is a channel of the supply chain which adds the value of time and place utility"

"Business language doesn't change as quickly, but logistics and supply chains are interchanged far too frequently to try and separate the meaning. In its broadest terms, Supply Chain is more strategic and external to your company; Logistics is more tactical and internal to your company."

"It's commonly accepted that Supply Chain Management is part of the wider concept of logistics and not another term for it. While logistics is generally accepted to cover the whole process from A-Z, SCM is the management of upstream activities into the organization to a point determined by the organizations structure."

"Logistics is, the movement of material between trading partners: Vendor to Company, Company to Customer. In other words, the transportation element."

"Supply Chain is managing all of the material movement related to the trading partners: Visibility to Vendor Inventory, Ordering from Vendor, Receipts from Vendors, Storage, Production/Sales Order Fulfillment, Loading, In-Transit Visibility, Visibility to Customer Inventory and Ordering from the Customer"

"There is the need to manage that supply chain. This involves 5 distinct competency sets, namely:

1. Production & Inventory Control
2. Strategic Procurement
3. Transportation & Storage
4. Information Systems
5. Improvement

When these are operated together holistically and in unison, we have supply chain management (SCM) - call it logistics if you like, but it does not change the nature of the activities"

"Supply Chain Management is the discipline related to the management of the planning, manufacturing and operations necessary to bring a product to the market place, from the sourcing of materials through to the delivery of the completed product. From the above definition, you clearly see that Logistics management is embedded in SCM....!"

"Logistics definition is a structured activity based function of managing inventories and moving parts from point A to point B. Whereas supply chain is a set of functions across multiple departments including supply management, inventory management, information flows across all apply points and all the way till the customer receives the product."

"Definition of Supply Chain Management
Supply chain management encompasses the planning and management of all activities involved in sourcing and procurement, conversion, and all logistics management activities. Importantly, it also includes coordination and collaboration with channel partners, which can be suppliers, intermediaries, third party service providers 3PL's – 4PL's and customers. In essence, supply chain management integrates supply and demand management within and across companies."

"Definition of Logistics Management

Logistics management is that part of supply chain management that plans, implements, and controls the efficient, effective forward and reverses flow and storage of goods, services and related information between the point of origin and the point of consumption in order to meet customers' requirements."

"Logistics Management is the management of the flow of goods and services between the point of origin and the point of consumption in order to meet the requirements of customers. It involves the integration of information transportation, inventory, warehousing, material handling, and packaging, and often security. It is part of the SCM which adds the value of time and place utility."

"Supply chain management (SCM) is the management of a network of interconnected businesses involved in the ultimate provision of product and service packages required by end customers it involves the "design, planning, execution, control, and monitoring of the supply chain activities with the objective of creating net value, building a competitive infrastructure, leveraging worldwide logistics, synchronizing supply with demand and measuring performance globally. In Short SCM is the General and comes up with the ideas, customer needs etc. and then monitors.

Logistics makes it work per SCM guide lines."

> Footnote: Above are edited comments as found on the internet from a variety of professionals.

PART ONE

The Start in Sales

Let go of

Old beliefs

Expand new ideas

Attract new business

Use new approaches

Maximize your Sales

How come some are so unprofessional?

I was working for Char-Broil (yes, I became really good at BBQ grilling as well) a well established company based in Columbus, Georgia. I was responsible for the overall supply chain from a logistics and transportation point of view. In those days less people knew the real importance of a well functioning supply chain although I personally always treated it as that the company could not function without a great supply chain.

During this time I had the opportunity to meet a large number of transportation sales executives.

I got the normal sales call from an ocean freight sales representative. I accepted the appointment and he came in to present his company and hopefully obtain our business.

Granted he was relatively young and inexperienced but that should not be an excuse for being unprepared. He vaguely knew a few things about us and I was forced to spend a good amount of time educating him on our company and our products as well as our locations. To my astonishment he knew almost as little about his own company and he had a very difficult time positioning the need for his services. I listened to his sales pitch and thought, how come he is so unprofessional and unprepared in his presentation?

Needless to say, he did not make it back for a follow up call nor did I invite him to create a proposal. My point is that if he would have taken the time to at least read up and get informed about the company he would have had some success.

The other side of this argument lies in the fact that I didn't really know them either and had I taken the time educate myself about his company the meeting could have been successful or wouldn't have taken place at all.

We both wasted a lot of time and as we all know the commodity of time is shrinking.

So what can we do to better understand each other and collaborate?

The real secret lies in combining marketing in a new way to refocus your personal and company position and to put more energy into your preparation. Once you do this your personal commitment and attainment of your professional goals will increase tremendously. The old phrase, prepare, prepare and present still holds true.

"Hold yourself responsible for a higher standard than anybody expects of you."

-Henry Becker

If you live by this, and are privy to proper training, you have every reason to succeed and go further than you thought possible!

Knowledge and believing in your ability is the KEY!

Knowledge comes from learning and experience, the ability to apply such knowledge at any time to the appropriate supply chain situations will be the key to success. You need proper training, good leadership and a firm understanding of your product to be ultimately successful in supply chain sales.

Ask yourself:

> How is your attitude, are you positive enough to handle rejection?
>> This comes with discipline and commitment and isn't always so easy.
> Some say 50% of people that fail in sales do so because of a bad or improper ATTITUDE.
> Are you persistent enough?
> Do you have a sense of humor
>> Being funny is one thing, but how you see things is the real key.
>> Can you create the feeling of "you made my day" from a customer; sometimes a good sense of humor can do this – can you?
> Sales is about relationships, can you build them and maintain them?

This list is almost endless and I have only attempted to address a few of the most vital questions. I recommend you seriously evaluate your own personal answers to these questions and possibly rate yourself accordingly. Are you willing to learn from your past mistakes and improve yourself and your performance to ultimately increase your level of success? (This takes self criticism and is not as easy at it might first appear).

The invisible fence

This is an old term (probably older then I am…), it makes a reference to the actual sales "barrier" between the sales representative and the customer of the services and or products that are being sold. An example of the two sides of the "fence" would be a 3PL's (third party logistics provider) warehousing service being sold to a manufacturing or ecommerce company.

It is from both sides of this "invisible" fence I will be providing you with insights as to how important it is to understand each others' side.

I have the dubious honor (for lack of a better word) to have worked both sides of this invisible fence. I have been a sales person but also been on the other side receiving the pitch and listening to why I should make the deal.

Being in sales was something I always wanted to do.

I personally started in sales in a very harsh manner.

I spent over ten years in actual operations for several global supply chain, logistics and parcel companies. I suddenly, one day, realized there was not much more that I could learn in operations and thought it would be of a greater benefit to the company and to me if I were in sales. I could really make a difference so I became a sales executive.

Since my sales experience was very limited, except for the fact that my telephone exposure to our customers had been very extensive, I really had to start from the beginning. We simply had no sales training or sales books available so it would be a rather harsh start.

My boss told me that my first sales call would be to a specific customer which he knew. We were, at this time, not handling any business for them and I would not need an appointment all I had to do was just to walk in and introduce myself. Being inexperienced and not willing to object at this time, I agreed. I entered the customers' offices and introduced myself then asked to see the person my boss told me was the right contact party. Immediately, as my new (and first) business card was handed to him, he came storming out of his office. He proceeded to insult my company and me with every four letter word he could possibly find to put us down. What my boss did not tell me was the fact that we had a small contract with this company which simply went wrong from the beginning to end and caused this customer to (obviously) get the wrong impression of our company. To receive this kind of insult from someone (with a very red face and screaming at top of his lungs) was certainly not my idea of sales, especially since this was my very first sales call.

Realizing I was too inexperienced to respond or try to provide a good explanation in this situation, I did the only reasonable thing I could think of which was to retreat (before the man physically threw me out). I went back to my office and made a complete analysis of this bewildering situation and managed to call the customer back to convince him to meet with me again.

We met, several days later; I explained in detail why things went wrong and what measures would have to be taken to make certain that this situation would not occur again. Two months later, after a few more meetings, we started to handle some business for this customer again.

No one should have to start out in sales this way, unprepared and thrown to the "sharks" in this fashion. My boss had but one thing in mind, if he (that's me) can survive this type of customer I will have a good sales executive who will take care of himself. The logic is somewhat sound behind this idea of having a tough sales representative who can work independently; however, there are better ways to "create" a good, professional sales executive.

RESEARCH AND PREPARATION FOR SALES

Don't assume that your customers or potential customers know:

- You, yourself
- Your company
- Your company's services and products

How to prepare yourself

You are part of the product and/or service you sell and you yourself will be the most important part of your presentation. As we have all heard, there is only one opportunity to make a first impression which is why it is imperative to make a very positive one on your first encounter with your customer.

Today's business world allows the majority of companies to have a more business casual attire and casual elegant clothing is typically accepted.

One 3PL company I know is one of the few companies that have not adapted to this way of thinking but remain at a more traditional dress code. They are firm on the fact that every one must be dressed in a dark suit and tie and female professionals in a similar fashion and regardless of customer they do not seem to conform to the dress code of most of their customers. Several of my customers have told me what a strange effect and impression it makes when a group of their executives and sales representatives come into a meeting room to see them.

There is absolute no issue with the fact that they are a formidable company and it has the respect of everyone, but this aspect is contradictory to most normal business rules. If you look at this from a message point of view, you could easily say that they are very professional and adheres to rules. On the other hand it also sends a message of not listening to the rest of the business community and if you elaborate on this aspect it would imply that they are also inflexible. This must be their way or no way. Add to the fact that if you have a group of five representatives at least 3 will open lap tops to take notes during the meeting. So not only do you have a conservative stern kind of look from them but you also have to put up with clutter from a number of laptops. Of course none of them have sufficient battery so they must look everywhere for electrical outlets. As you well know in many conference rooms those are under the table. So at this stage you will have three sales reps under the table competing for the electrical outlets. To say it is comical is certainly a truthful statement.

Since I personally have a lot of respect for their organization I will overlook this aspect and always listen to them.

Training is one thing that that they do well; all the reps would have been through a thorough training. The annoying part is that they are too trained and many of the sales statements are simply that; statements.

As an example they are trained to always ask for the total business, so even if the meeting is around a distinct issue or requirement, they will ask questions directly and immediately regarding the rest of the supply chain. Their training are in many cases adopted word by word by the rep and it is delivered this way. Word by word without emphasis and relevance to discussion of the topic at hand does not succeed. Enthusiasm is in many cases also lacking.

The impression is that they "must" ask this question and they are doing exactly what they are told. Well, this is great but before you ask this kind of question, you must first have listened to the customer needs and what they *really* need and want. Furthermore, the customer may not even be prepared to discuss any other aspect then what the reason for the appointment was, so do they understand the customer needs?

From the other side of the invisible fence this can be a very long meeting with many interruptions and discussions that has no relevance to the issue at hand. I am often asked to "control" meetings of this nature and setting an agenda is only step one. Some of my recommendations are to have a precursory discussion with the lead person or manager in charge. I will outline what needs to be discussed, the angle that has to be presented and how it is to be approached. I will not only give the agenda but I will outline areas that are not up for discussion. The illustration in this short story again amplifies the importance of knowing both sides.

For targeted training to be effective and to develop the necessary sales skills to reach the objective of obtaining new business it must be delivered in an effortless and natural way. This in itself takes development and strategic implementation of product characteristics, benefits, features and pricing structure. Success will follow to a much higher degree once the basic skill set is transferred to a sales rep. This will allow them to effectively deliver a value proposition that makes sense to a potential customer. Once it makes sense the trust factor can be established regardless if this is a small or large customer.

How do you create enthusiasm?

Why is enthusiasm even necessary, should it not be enough that you know your company, your industry and that alone will ensure your success?

My personal criteria for hiring anyone, rates enthusiasm and attitude right among the most important assets you can have. Sometimes you can also refer to this as passion and passionate people always have a higher degree of success.

Most sales people think they have a positive attitude, but they actually do not. This is a discipline that must be practiced on a regular basis. The essence is not a feeling that you have a positive attitude; it has to be a state of mind that is self induced. Your training and required skill set would have to be tailored to fit your organization.

Your approach could be different depending on the size of your company.

If you are employed by a small local company, you will obviously try to sell the local facilities. The local personnel and all their combined experience, knowledge and skill. If it is relevant to make a more global impression you should be in a position to outline your international network, infrastructure and of associates and contacts. There may be other special features you would need to stress, such as technology, future plans, special services, new products or services, present customers and personalized customer service. Under these circumstances it is imperative to create an impression of a trustworthy, well established and recognized service provider in your local community.

If, on the other hand your employer is a larger corporation with affiliations and/or their own offices throughout the world, this would be one of the main features you would highlight. The danger is much greater here because you assume your customer knows your company and its services just because you are from a well known firm. My point is, although your company may be well known, take nothing for granted go through your services and your products, explain and outline. As many established companies do, they assume you know nothing or maybe something. Regardless of the answer to those assumptions they made sure to ask as many questions as possible relevant or not. Another example would be that most people would associate FedEx with next day air envelopes and other similar services, but not all would know about their postal product or supply chain services.

How do you convey the awareness of your company?

This can be a difficult task at the best of times. One would assume that every one knows IBM, but they have expanded into services and consulting businesses that may not be as well known to the average executive. So even if you are IBM, UPS or FedEx don't forget to explain future expansions in relation to new types of services and products.

If you are privy to strategic development and strategies that your company have, the fact that you have made your customer aware, may influence them a year or more down the road as their long terms plans are being implemented. If you didn't inform them of your plans, you may not be part of your customers long term planning. Don't underestimate the importance of disclosing your long term planning to your customers, it may pay off handsomely over time.

So is the answer that most of us must become marketing specialists to be able to communicate the offerings of your company?

To turn a sales executive into a marketing executive, is in most cases very difficult, but this clearly illustrates the need for marketing to make sure the long term strategies are clear to the sales team. The sales team in itself will need proper training in how to bring this message to the customer. Even if you can create an interest in the long term growth plans of your company, it may be an invite to discuss in more details. Such invites usually involves senior executive management and is very desirable. To get to the decision makers of a potential customer to review your long term strategy is one way to increase your potential sales success.

SUMMARY STATEMENT:

If you don't know your product "inside and out," how will you be able to sell it successfully?

- The answer lies in research, research, preparation, preparation and presentation.
- Training is imperative but must be balanced to convey the correct amount of information and delivered at the right time.
- Know your customer before you even make the appointment. Try to understand where there is a real "need" for your product or service.
- Understand your competition and where their weaknesses are.

Sounds simple, but unless you are the best there is in explaining your product chances are the customer will consider your competition first. I firmly believe that personal enthusiasm and energy partly comes from a thorough knowledge of your product and when you visit a customer it will become visible. The tougher part is of course that competition is very intense and a large number of competitors have the same or similar services and products as you. This is why you and your personal enthusiasm will often do more then most of us think.

As strange as this may sound, even potential customers are human.

A personal relationship that you have developed with a customer will take you a long way. The deciding factor can most definitely become you and your personal behavior, your belief, enthusiasm in your product and the trust factor you personally convey.

I recently had a conversation with a Vice President of finance where she was presented with a choice of service providers in the auditing field. Two of the proposals were quite clearly after analysis the best choices with the best attributes and fees. I asked the simple question, what do you think, which one is actually the better one?

The answer was that her gut feeling suggested that the smaller company had the better product and service. I then asked her why do you prefer the smaller company, their fees are higher and their overall product offering is slightly below the other company. We evaluated some of the IS infrastructure features but that did not seem to be the reason. We also went through the decision matrix that I had created to assist in the process. Then she added, maybe it is because I thought that particular salesman, had a better presentation and frankly I liked him more. She was very honest about this and recognized that maybe she had hastened her decision process and allowed this aspect to weigh in prematurely and with too much emphasis.

What this illustrates is the importance of the personal representation and how the presentation is delivered. This actually becomes a personal impression as a base for the decision. The chance in many of these situations is that the choice is very much personal impressions and preferences are based on gut feeling.

In most negotiations, one of the most common strategies is to know your opponent in as much detail as possible. As you know by now, this book is written with the view so both sides of the fence can understand each other. It is also specifically a guide for the sales executives to pick up some ideas to correlate and better understand the other side. By knowing each others side, maybe we could cooperate and collaborate better to help each other to better outcomes and more successful relationships. Above all, could we save each other time and money?

It takes commitment, endurance, dedication, and courage to interact with a variety of customers to make a sale. Today people don't have time to waste, you need to act quickly and to the point to be successful.

From the other side of the "fence", you will develop a better understanding and appreciation for the overall sales process of the sales executive after you have heard their side of the "fence".

Here are some aspects from the other side of the invisible fence, to show what the sales executives are going through and this is "their world".

Sales Executive – his/her world

What makes a good sales executive, do you make them, mold them, train them or is it an evolution like no other?

Many sales people don't prepare at all which is a surefire way of becoming less successful. The old way of just walking in cold calling and receiving the handshake and welcome is quickly coming to an end so the need for preparation is essential.

Sometimes the expectation factor is driving behavior of sales people and it is very important to find out exactly what your management team/manager expects from a sales representative on a day to day basis.

For example;

- **Do they want you to make four sales visits per day or more?**
- **Do you have a quota to be met?**
- **Is it imperative to write a report on every visit or how are these reporting requirements structured?**
- **What should your goal setting be like to be realistic?**
- **How do you balance your commission (if you receive one) to your sales efforts and how is new sales balanced with maintenance sales?**

REPORTING FORMATS FOR SUPPLY CHAIN EXECUTIVES

Many managers are "report happy" which creates an abundance of work and information that simply is not necessary.

The different reporting segments should be for daily, weekly and monthly reports.

There are obviously a large number of variations of important information that can be tailored to fit each company's requirements.

Take a look at such software packages that have task management and project management modules.

In today's market closing a sale on the first call or after the first number of emails is highly unlikely, so a time management list is important. Since the time line often is long don't forget to write down how interested the potential customer was, who on their team seemed receptive and when to make a new appointment. Write all important tasks down, set prompts in your database and calendars, don't rely on your memory for every detail, you can lose a customer over just not remembering to do something!

SALES FORCE AUTOMATION

There are several sales force automation packages available today. The benefits are significant and you should strive to become an expert in using these tools. If it is true that 78% of sales time is NOT spent on selling this kind of software tools should be justifiable. Most of these tools are accessible via a mobile app and will give you access to all or selected company data. They allow you to organize data in such modules as access to CRM (Customer Relationship Management) or WMS (Warehouse Management System) for inventory and product availability. Within some of these tools you will find processes that automate your sales course of action which could include selling phases, email reminders, various selling activities and documents. Task and activity management tools are important and lately social media interaction is an option in selected packages. WebEx and live chat are available on some of these tools as well.

Sales force automation software has a large numbers of features such as a dashboard, lead generating and rating capabilities. The dashboards are used to analyze progress, lead and work in synch with Outlook and Google Apps. Depending on how you configure these tools you can also have access to other sales teams and company progress thus making you more aware of events and opportunities.

Microsoft has also created a Sales Force Automation tool with the latest version bundled in the Dynamics CRM software collection called Outlook Client Experience. As the name suggest it is indeed compatible with outlook and can be synchronized just like your mobile device. Oracle Siebel CRM, Salesforce.com, ACT! By Sage, Sugar CRM, Batchbook.com and Landslide are a few others.

iphone, Blackberry, Droid etc...

I know it is a blessing... OR is it a curse?

Always being available and reachable is a good thing, but you need to balance and making sure that being available makes sense considering the business situation. To always monitor your phone for emails is an important task, but when do you stop?

I recently had the opportunity to work with a sales professional from a Global 3PL. He was the ultimate in being available at all times. We dealt with China and an ocean and air import program for one of my clients so being available late at night made some sense. He needed real time interaction with China and this would be the best time he could get it. He was always there and we successfully maneuvered around a very stressed and sensitive client that really did not understand how the supply chain works. He just needed constant updates of even the most minuscule detail. He was one of those micro managers that just would not trust anyone to do the job right. For this customer it was the right thing to be available at these hours.

Given another client with different criteria, being available during evening hours may not have been required.

I suggest that when you obtain a new customer, find out how they have need of information and when it is appropriate to return with proper information.

It still needs to be confirmed that for real emergency you or someone on your team is always available.

This process needs to be established within your own company as well as for customers.

I believe that everyone appreciates that we all have private lives to live and this should be respected from both sides of the fence.

SUMMARY STATEMENT:

Once you have established exactly what your company expects of you and how you have to advise them of your activities, you are on the way. It is imperative to understand the reporting system within your company, verbal and written because without this knowledge you could end up in un-deserved trouble.

At this stage you know your product, your company and all its services "inside and out" and you are very familiar with the reporting systems.

FINDING SALES LEADS

Possibly one of the most time consuming tasks in sales.

Everybody talks about networking and how important this is and I agree. It is sometimes surprising how many people you know and how many people they in turn know. Let your network know what you and your company does.

One of the obvious places to network and look in is always inside your own company. Meet and discuss with the different operations, sales and marketing managers. Find out for which customers we do not handle all business or only sell a limited number of products and services to.

Ask the operations managers to provide you with an opportunity to look through records and familiarize yourself with all clients. Find out if there are some customers that could benefit from a maintenance sales call. Maintenance sales calls are extremely important and should be scheduled, which I will further outline in a different chapter. Pay special attention to any customer that only appears once or twice, or suddenly doesn't use your company services. Those clients are a must to contact to simply find out why there hasn't been anymore business from them. Another good habit to develop is to discuss with other sales representatives if there are any customers that would benefit by a visit from you. Maybe your expertise in the area you know best can be of help since the sales representative presently calling on the customer is predominantly concerned with another area. After all, we are all on the same team and team effort is a significant contributor to the overall success of your company.

Discuss in detail with your manager or vice president if there are any clients they can think of who were active in the past but have disappeared. There could also be other clients that they are aware of who may be dealing with the competition.

Don't forget to ask, it is quite often the only way to find out.

Depending on how your company is organized, there may be databases that can be sorted with customer activity, service used, invoiced value, frequency and many other criteria that would make sense in your world.

The opportunities of finding sales leads in-house are extremely good and should be explored to their fullest potential.

- Don't stop with the in-house search for sales leads after you have done it once, do it on a regular basis.

Obtain access to any company databases from accounting and any other documentary correspondence that would make sense.

Don't forget that thing called the web.....

Explore some of the old fashion things as well such as industry web sites, trade publications or magazines. Newspapers always provide a good source for sales leads or that news flash on Yahoo. Look for published appointments of personnel. If you see a company who is looking for supply chain people be it for export, shipping, warehouse workers or managers in any logistics capacity, don't hesitate, follow up. This could mean that this company is very busy shipping or handling large inventories, which could indicate an area of opportunity for you regardless which area of the supply chain you service.

BE ALERT when you are driving and if traffic permits, check out businesses sometimes just seeing a name will ignite that special thought or simply remind you of something....

Social Media, what is it?

What is it, how is it defined?

Social Media is a complex, organic online conversation, which makes it involving, empowering and demonstrative!!

From a business sales point of view, the first look may be that this area seems not to be for me; after all it is more "social" and personal.

However when you recognize that 73% of people are blog users, 45% have their own blog, 39% subscribes to a RSS feed and

47% says that social media influences their decision. This means that a customer would read a posted view of consumer goods or services and then make an "informed" decision to purchase or not.

Networking on the web is imperative, design a plan and follow it.

Assuming that that these statistics also hold true in the Supply Chain world, I would suggest taking a closer look at these websites.

Who hasn't heard of Twitter and if used properly, you can create quite a following.

LinkedIn is probably the premier site for business leads and both you and your company should be listed. The trick here is to be active and to participate in discussions and create discussions. People will see you and may remember that you can help them with a pressing issue or provide a service.

Social media has the ability to generate exposure, create income traffic, build relationships, bring in new leads and not to forget that social media has a higher conversion rate to a sale then traditional marketing.

To be successful in social media you would need to become serious about your effort and follow a few basic steps to increase your chances to become successful.

Here are some suggestions

1. Create a strategy and follow through which in most cases should mean to try to best identify your potential customer.

2. Establish a presence; in case of LinkedIn you must create a complete profile. Plaxo is a lesser known and used site, with lesser competition. Another couple of lesser know sites are, biznik.com and Merchantcircle.com who are more of local community networking sites which you can use to connect and promote your own business locally.

If you didn't know how to use Facebook for business, take a closer look. It is possible to configure a business Facebook , where your business associates can view your content and messages.

3. Nurture relationships, simply said keep in touch, update with promotional statements.

4. Maintain your presence and update virtually everyday. This means participate in groups, discussion, update your own events and profile as appropriately.

Let's face it, all this information is absolutely useless unless you take the time to follow up and actually make that initial telephone call or e-mail to evaluate these potential opportunities.

Evaluation of sales leads

Now you have some sales leads, but you don't know too much about your potential customers. How much time do you realistically spend before you contact a customer?

The internet is naturally the first place to go to see if they have a website or if there are messages and articles about their company. LinkedIn is an obvious choice since almost everyone is listed here. This will also give you access to the names of potential direct client contacts. To find the email address or even the phone number is sometimes difficult so you can additionally subscribe to a data base with this type of information. You can access databases or subscribe to them where Hoover is probably the most comprehensive one. I have found several very useful and up to date and not expensive data bases with email and phone numbers so there are options.

Once you have this basic information you can decide if you need to spend more time to make sure you understand and know enough about this company to approach them.
Remember, you don't want to waste your time or the time of the person on the other side of the invisible fence.

The appointment

On one side of the fence it can be annoying to get the call from a sales rep but on the other side it may be exactly what you have been looking for, so most of us take the call. I must say that the courtesy of taking an outside call has been dramatically reduced and receiving no or little response is not uncommon.

From the other side of the invisible fence if you don't make the call how can you get the appointment and make the deal?

As I have stated before when you do make the call it is imperative to know something about the company. If you have acquired pertinent information about the company, you will stand out and chances are the person you are calling will spend a little extra time with you. Besides I personally believe it demonstrates some good sense and shows respect for your potential client's busy day. A good potential client will also quickly ask you about your knowledge of the company. If you can confirm you know something about their company this early in the conversation, your chance to give your sales pitch will increase.

This will significantly improve your chances to obtain that valuable appointment. An important rule is to sell the appointment first, not the service or product offering, that will come later.

I have often used an odd number when asking if they have time to talk. For example, do you have two minutes and 39 seconds? If the person on the other end has any sense of humor, you will get a positive response which will increase the effectiveness of your sales pitch and set the tone for the total conversation and follow up. Make notes of your conversations, so you will remember what was said, and most important make certain you obtain the person's name and title for future reference. So now you got their <u>attention</u>, you need to outline a <u>specific service</u> you intend to sell. Since you already have done some research you should be able to identify a potential need maybe in the warehousing and distribution area. You need to ask a number of leading questions to establish exactly where in the supply chain your solution is needed. Once you have established this, you have gained their <u>interest</u>. This is your opportunity to pinpoint the services that they would need. Be brief but as specific as you can without giving too much information. You have to make them want to hear more and this is not be the time to sell but merely create an interest and need for these services. Once you are at this stage you must get the <u>commitment</u> for the appointment which is the main purpose for this call.

The key in this approach is to be enthusiastic and informative. You must create enough interest for them to perceive that this is an opportunity that has clear benefits to them.

Another good way to get that appointment is to ask for HELP!! This is sometimes very difficult, but is a very powerful way to proceed, since most people want to help.

- Asking for help when calling for the appointment is sometimes the only way to find out who to approach. I have often simply asked the receptionist and then asked for the person responsible for the type of service I was selling. Once told, instead of requesting to be put through I would request the assistant and ask some qualifying questions.
  - o The same kind of approach can also be used if you do a cold call and merely drop in to see the receptionist. Sometimes just asking for information may take you further then you think?
  - o Assistants and receptionists are there to help and be a vital communication link to the management.
- Of course, we can also access the web on the iphone so a cold call doesn't have to be completely "cold".

Most importantly in all sales and especially telephone sales, don't interrupt your customer, LISTEN. One of the most significant parts of sales is to establish a personal relationship with your customer, get to know your customer, let him get to know and trust you. So once you have the appointment or a request for a call back to continue this conversation, <u>don't forget</u> to call back and make sure your notes are current.

"Needless to say, I am not one of them."

-D.H. Laurence

Even if this person "avoids" you and postpones you for two or three months at a time, always call back and make reference to your last call and what you wanted to talk about. Soon you will create name recognition and be known by your name. I talked to one customer in this fashion for at least three months and besides being known by my name I also was labeled as "the freight guy". A customer with a sense of humor is worth a tremendous amount. I did obtain that crucial appointment where he decided to see the "freight guy" and because he already "knew" me he immediately agreed to see a comprehensive quotation. I obtained the business only on the second actual visit. This is a prime example of how telephone sales can work for you to speed up the process.

You have an appointment, now what?

Knowing your potential prospect and their business before you make the sales call, is the overall idea but sometimes we don't follow our own rules.

1.   Walk in, hope for the best, ask a lot of questions and promote your product as much as you can and try to get to the point where you can present a price and/or a quotation. Does this not sound like "throwing a dart" approach or a cold call?

Of course, we have all done this and keep on doing this. Although, I have always believed enthusiasm sells, under these circumstances, you will have to have a lot of enthusiasm…

2.   Examine your new appointment; make sure you have enough information on the company, is this the decision maker or do you have to "go through" this person to get to the real decision maker? Angle your presentation towards the person you are meeting with i.e., if you are meeting with a junior level executive make a presentation that is more in line with their duties and responsibilities and perhaps you will have to meet their superior to obtain this business. In the event you have an appointment with an accountant or purchasing manager price does become important and you have to make your presentation price sensitive.

3.   I have found it very helpful to at the beginning of the appointment ask how much time he or she can spare you during this

first meeting. Once you have established this you can arrange and schedule your presentation accordingly. Here again, you have established the areas of more exact concern during your telephone contact and can accurately target a specific service or need that this company has. If you don't know what they need, make a shorter introduction with general descriptions and leading questions as to what kind of services and products they may require. This will give you an opportunity to fill in and apply additional sales pitches.

4.   If you can find out who your competition is (which you definitely must and your knowledge of the competition is imperative) you can further target your presentation and come closer to introducing a proposal.

5.   Try to be memorable in your meeting with the customer, take a creative idea to each sales call.

I was at a customers office and a sales rep had made an appointment with my client. The rep promised no more then 30 minutes but failed to identify what my client might need in form of his services. He had a wonderful presentation of his company and went through the PowerPoint presentation with a lightning type of speed. He was well rehearsed and what he sold made perfect sense. Only one thing wrong with this, my client had no need for this service. My client is a very nice person and did not want to offend this sales rep so he decided to listen. We had however prior to the meeting agreed that if this was not of interest I would step in and close down the presentation. After a few minutes into his presentation I stopped and re-directed him to an area that possibly would be of interest to my client. He took a few minutes on that topic and then went back to the PowerPoint.

He obviously did not listen or he was too trained to keep going through the presentation hoping that something would stick. I interrupted again and provided some further direction and advised that if we see no interest or opportunity in this next area, I would stop any further presentation. Once again, he made a brief detour into the area of interest and then went back to the generic PowerPoint presentation. At that time I firmly closed down the sales presentation and explained his services were not required.

I later met this sales rep at a convention and took him aside to explain you cannot be this disrespectful of a potential customer's time. A sales call must have an element of mutual respect and not be a sales pitch with a hope of discovering a need during the presentation. He confessed he thought the company could use his services and since the company is a large corporation with national name recognition, he thought he knew enough about the company. In so many words I conveyed *thinking* that you know a company is far from *knowing* that you understand what a potential client could need.

The reason I tell this story is because if we had worked together, from both sides of the fence, at the time of making the appointment much time and effort could have been saved.

Raising the awareness of asking those few extra questions at time of the first contact needs to be done.

How do you decide if a client is important enough?

Should you go and visit this company or is the business potential simply too small and an email will suffice? This is a very

difficult item since sometimes a small company can become very big, and if you have helped them from a small size to become a large company, chances are you can establish and maintain a long term relationship.

I received a sales lead from an overseas colleague in Germany who had visited with a local shoe manufacturer. The manufacturer told him that one shoe store in my city had bought ten pairs of shoes at a recent exhibition and indicated an interest in becoming their national distributor. When I heard of this, I called the shoe store and the gentleman had a tremendous amount of questions. He was very excited about his new shoes, and I agreed to visit with him. Once at his store we started discussing importation process and how to get his shoe quota for customs. As we were discussing this in the store a lady comes in and wanted to purchase a navy blue pair of shoes. Not willing to miss a sale, he excused himself and went to show the lady shoes. After about eleven pairs she found a pair that she really liked but she insisted they must be navy blue. He had no nave blue but he had black. He started to explain he had none but the lady was very insisting. I could see the frustration coming on and the lady became more adamant about the navy color. He then stood up and said I may have a pair in the back that would be just right for you. He then brought in a pair of black, yes black shoes. The difference was he explained elaborately that these were actually "navy black" shoes and so close in color that no one could tell them apart and they would look just great on her.

His "navy black" sales pitch was so effective the lady became excited about her new "navy black" shoes and purchased them immediately. My opinion was that if he can sell "navy black" shoes, he must be a great salesman and quite capable of selling "regular" colored shoes. I initially spent a lot of time with this gentleman and he started to import small air freight shipments. My company handled the complete supply chain from Germany through customs cleared and delivered to his shoe store. The interest in his shoes grew at a very rapid speed and the shipments became increasingly larger (and more profitable). Before long, he sold his shoe store and became an independent shoe distributor for the whole country.

His logistics and supply chain requirements continued to grow and he eventually became one of the largest shoe importers. Since I initially helped him get started, I had a personal relationship with him that maintained this account with my company for a very long time.

- **My advice is to evaluate very carefully before you discard any new or small company that you contact, you just never know what will happen.**

EXCELLENCE IN CUSTOMER SERVICE

The moment of truth

This is a statement that is commonly used by many customer sales specialists:

Q: What is the moment of truth in our industry?

A: Every time one of our employees is in contact with a customer for what ever reason. Further defined this is when a customer, internal or external make a decision about you or form an opinion about you, your company, your services based on their interaction with anyone from your front line including CEO.

The moment of truth is often correlated with excellence in customer service. One of the most common remarks in this regard is the fact that your customer service is "only as strong as your weakest employee". If one of our employees is unprofessional in his/her manner, it will indeed reflect negatively upon the whole company. We all expect our employees to exercise "common sense" and be courteous. We also know that it is not enough to simply *expect* this from our employees or of yourself as a sales executive. We all have our "bad" days when the stress (and there is plenty of this commodity in our industry) has been extraordinary and it is easy to brush off a customer and not give them the time you normally would have given. Unless you have a personality and experience that can effectively deal with this aspect of customer contact, you will have to receive professional training.

Is the customer always right? The answer is yes, and if you don't agree, please read the question again and adapt the answer.

There are many ways to assist your customer and we must always do our best to LISTEN to the real problem of a specific situation and related requirements.

Why are your customers calling?

Is it because of problems or issues or is the flow of information not being presented to your customer in a complete and timely manner, or what?

Once you have established and analyzed the data provided, you will have to come up with a solution which can satisfy your customer, or provide an answer which will adequately justify the fact, "the customer is always right."

Commonly these type of scenarios fall into three categories, people, process and technology. If it is as a people issue this most be addressed immediately and solved maybe by training or increased customer service efforts. A process and technology issue often provides for some time since it may require intervention of a number of people. This doesn't mean you can delay to take action nevertheless the most important task here is that you communicate what you intend to do. You will need to provide an estimated outline of the time and end result.

The moment of truth is extremely strong and even a slight mishap or lack of effort could lose a customer quickly.

Maintenance sales – client retention, why do it?

How important is it really? When I have been talking to professionals in the supply chain industry it seems most agree that this is of utmost importance. I found that it is common to hear from executives that at least 60-70% of all sales activities should be concentrated on maintenance sales. "After all the competition is fierce and we must keep in contact with our customers."

Change, is what drives the maintenance sales. Your customer changes and so does their needs and actual requirements. The truth is most supply chain companies recognize that they must do maintenance sales however this portion is not always well organized. This means that we meet with our customers but we do not "perform" the visit that could be classified as a maintenance call. One of the most important issues to address in maintenance sales is the simple question of "am I talking to the right person(s)"?

The only way to arrive at a level of comfort in maintenance sales is to systematically arrange and analyze your customers. I recommend that you create a data base or some sort of program or work with an annual calendar and discuss in a sales meeting each of your customers needs. Make sure to regularly include your operations management in the sales meetings since they deal with the customers on a daily basis. Create a "must report back" system and assign one employee (sales executive, operations manager, supervisor, vice president, etc.) to make that "Maintenance call" to every single customer that you have. Decide in the same meeting (or the next one) if an actual visit is necessary or if a telephone call is satisfactory. Create an individual call list with dates for each person. Further design a follow up system and reporting format that confirms that each person has indeed followed up as agreed. Send reminders to associates that "forget" or who are procrastinating the contact and make sure that no customer is missed. It is imperative for the company's survival that this is followed through properly.

What is a maintenance call?

Is it enough to call your customer and just be his friend and take him to lunch and get along famously. Well, many of us have been through this kind of situation and they do serve a good purpose, however, it is absolutely imperative to ask direct questions. Questions that pertain to the performance of the company's services, rates, personnel and our attention to their essential needs.

- Have we made any mistakes lately?
- How did we correct our mistakes?
- Did anyone else whose services we employed (for sub services or farmed out to other contractors, etc.) perform to their standards?

Don't forget to ask your customer how their company is changing. For instance:

- Do they have new products that have to be shipped?
- New packaging requirements?
- New markets that will be entered?
- New vendor sources for raw material?
- New importing lanes, air or ocean?
- New System requirements that we may have to integrate with?
- Is our communication and information flow adequate and meet your needs?
- What have we done right or provided great service?
- Multi channel sales
- Ecommerce, B2B or B2C?
  - Does it require an independent supply chain?
  - Delivery services – UPS, FedEx, DHL or USPS?

There are indeed a lot of hard honest questions that must be asked, and I recommend to formulate and go through these types of questions with everyone involved in the maintenance sales program. Make sure your maintenance personnel and yourself are totally comfortable and understand the importance of these types of questions.

Typically there are discrepancies between intended and actual provided service and a LACK of complaints may not always be the best situation. There will be a time when we will not like the answers we are receiving and we honestly think the customer is wrong. Please re-read the question above "is the customer always right?" We do know that answer!

Never confuse a maintenance call with a "regular" conversation or visit. A maintenance call MUST accomplish precisely what it was designed to achieve. It is probably the most important customer service contact you'll make; one that will save your long term relationship and ensure your entire business foundation is firm.

> **No news is good news is not true in maintenance sales.**

One of my personal mottos has always been and remains to this day,

"As long as my customers talk to me we can resolve the issues. It is when we don't talk or communicate that I start to worry".

Please always try to take action before the situation gets out of control by discussing the issues at hand. Virtually any situation can be resolved by communicating.

A number of years ago, I made a maintenance sales visit to one of my customers. They utilized our air freight services from Europe, after the usual "warm up" conversation, I started to ask specific questions:

> How is your cargo arriving from France?
> Is it on time?
> Do we rate the house airway bills and bills of ladings correctly?
> Are there any charges on the bills that you do not understand, or that you think are unwarranted or need an explanation?
> How is the customs clearance?
> The rate of exchange?

I always ask specific questions, although it is sometimes an area which you do not wish to discuss since you may be adding a little "extra" on. For example, the rate of exchange to make supplementary profit and have a slight mark up or be based on a rate of exchange that is influenced on past deviations. Don't avoid, these type of questions be frank and honest because if you don't your competition most certainly will. They will highlight these items and use the answers against you. I know because I have successfully used this technique on many occasions.

The times in the supply chain and logistics industry where "you could get away with that extra profit margin" is gone. We have a much more educated customer today, and the professional standards in our own industry have increased considerably. Competition provides for a higher quality business environment and the actual profits are realistically accepted by the customers. After all, it is still OK to make a healthy profit, because if you can't generate a good bottom line income you simply cannot afford to provide good service in the long term. Good service is one of the back bones of our industry. We are not unlike any other industry and must always strive to provide top service.

As important as maintenance sales is, it may never be so over powering that we forget to approach and sell to new customers. One other important angle to look at when considering new sales techniques and maintenance sales is to evaluate if this is an acceptable practice from a customer's point of view.

New customers guarantee a certain level of growth, and established customers' guarantees a certain level of stability and foundation. This is the criteria required for any company to strategically create a viable future. The balance between these two activities has to be decided upon by each management team in conjunction with both sales and operations personnel. It is, however, imperative that the "team spirit" is working, and the format for sales strategy is accepted and understood. You have to make certain that you have the highest possible level of support from ALL levels within your company.

"Without involvement, there is no commitment"

-Steven R. Covey

How to design a maintenance plan

After my previous comments on maintenance sales it is time to develop the maintenance plan. Since virtually everyone agrees that maintenance sales or customer retention is of utmost importance; I will briefly elaborate further on the benefits of a properly designed maintenance plan. Let me make the statement that maintenance sales and customer service should be closely related and the information must be cross-referenced. Never replace the customer service, in any aspect, with maintenance sales or vice versa. For example, your feed back from maintenance sales activities will give you very important information as to the actual design of your customer service program. It will allow you to create training for your "front line" staff and other selected personnel to bring competence levels up in areas where your customers feel you are weak. The design of your maintenance plan should, by the same token, be created partially from feed back and obtained from daily customer service contacts. It is a very good idea to design a system where information can flow back and be properly evaluated. Naturally, you can create a "monster" system that will quickly become non-functional. Instead, try to select certain areas that are of critical concern in your day to day business activities.

One such area of critical concern would be accounts receivable. If your cash flow is poor your whole company can suffer. As a sales executive, you may from time to time be requested to contact your customers to speed up payment of old invoices. It will be a matter of balancing your own requirements against your good relation ship to ensure payment without friction.

To estimate what it will take to provide the most beneficial customer service plan and to assess the actual cost, is a difficult task at all times, but it must be done. When going through the process of creating a maintenance plan you will have to evaluate other areas of concern such as creating a structure for quality and a continuous improvement process. This process must provide guidelines on how you can interact with your customers in this respect.

You should find a solution to implement as an interactive collaboration with your customers. The areas of immediate concern, in establishing this system, are to develop a good way of setting priorities for different functions as well as evaluating actual software systems and other related databases. Most importantly, it is a matter of deciding on how to arrange your personnel resources, who to put in management positions, who should interact with selected customers, and where the levels of empowerment should be drawn. For example, should you empower a front-line customer sales representative to reduce an incorrect invoice, and issue a credit note based on the information available at the time of initial customer contact? There are numerous instances where these factors will have to be evaluated and decided upon in order to maximize your customer service and interaction with your own customers. To identify a few contact points of critical concern you would have to evaluate:

➢ What is visible to the customer and what back up support should not be visible?

➢ How to optimize delivery at contact points (training of representatives)?

➢ What is the customer's perception of your company?

You must also design your maintenance plan in such a fashion that your questions will reveal something about your customers current and future plans. This knowledge alone will in turn provide you with many tools you need to customize your approach and meet their requirements. I have always tried to get the customer personally involved in a project where they actually become a part of the solution. A good example in involving your customer in this process would be the design of packaging to fit into a special transportation container. Any IT systems enhancement process is a very good project although it can be time consuming and at times irritating (why does it take so long, yes most IT departments are the same…). Maybe the design of an assembly process or pick line in a warehouse could be altered to fit better. Maybe the mix in the inventory has changed and the original inventory for the 80/20 rule is outdated. It could be something as simple as arranging the actual availability of high cube containers. Additional areas of interaction could be another way of prioritizing service levels or to identify their specific requests. Regardless of the task or issues to be resolved with your customer any level of involvement will pave the way for a better understanding and a closer, stronger bond.

Basically, you have to use your maintenance sales to understand your customer and their requirements. You have to "pinpoint", what has to be performed over and above the usual call of duty and work this into an action plan.

By asking the right questions you can really see it from the customers side (always try to put yourself in their shoes) and link your dedicated maintenance representatives and sales or customer service representatives directly to the customer in question. This brings the issue of quality and how to measure quality into direct focus. Interaction with your customer in this matter is imperative.

You have to decide to what degree you want to interact with your customer, determine where it becomes a "natural way", and where it becomes a burden, simply over worked and too time consuming and costly. What are the real barriers in this matter? Do they pose a threat or is it an opportunity (in disguise)?

Regardless, you must have systems in place to measure:

- **Performance**
- **Reliability**
- **Durability**
- **How quality is perceived by your customers?**
- **Your performance standards and how to set them**

Most importantly you have to identify the methods of how to manage change and improvement as well as understanding what flexibility you should apply to each customer.

When and how do you "turn a customer over to the operations departments' staff or contact person?

This is indeed a delicate question and there is no real universal answer to this. As a guideline I would suggest that this aspect become an integral part of your meetings concerning maintenance sales. A gradual "withdrawal" is quite often the most accepted way of delegating a customer to the operations departments. Another well accepted format is to make "joint" visits with your operations person to make a formal introduction. However, you have to be careful not to give the impression that you are out of the picture and actually not interested in your customers relationship anymore. I have successfully, explained to customers that I will not be directly involved in day to day routines. However, I will be immediately accessible in case of any problems, or if there are any new types of services required.

The "Switch factor"

Once your customer is part of the process, he will become part of the solution. He will be much less likely to leave you and it will be more difficult for your competition to obtain any business from this customer. I have often referred to a customer's likelihood of leaving you as the "switch factor." If the "switch factor" is low your risk of losing the customer is minimal. You must do everything possible to reduce this "switch factor" and analyze the associated risk factors.

One other term commonly used in this matter is to create "golden handcuffs" on your customers. Maybe it is more accurately to state that these "golden handcuffs" should be <u>with</u> your customer since a true partnership is really what is desired. I think this term is well understood and it accurately illustrates a close bond between you and your customers. These "golden handcuffs" can be in the form of systems interconnectivity whereas it is time consuming and potentially expensive to disengage. Regardless, you must know your customer and their requirements intimately and preferably ahead of time. If you can achieve this, you have the opportunity of becoming pro-active and not re-active. This could indeed mean the difference in maintaining a customer. After all, the more information you have in this respect, the better you can organize yourself. By being better organized you can tailor your services and rates to achieve maximum customer satisfaction at a minimum cost. It is a known fact, that the more information you have about a certain customer, the less physical time you will require for preparation of a proposal. This will reduce the actual re-work time and effort to produce the best possible proposal.

A final statement on maintenance sales and customer service is, that if you don't have a well designed maintenance plan and do not perform maintenance sales with the right questions, you will never know how your company is performing until it is too late!

Value added services, what is it?

Probably the most used and abused statement in our industry and in many others as well.

> ➤ **What is it really?**
> ➤ **Should we promote it?**
> ➤ **Is it new or have we been doing this all along but never really put a label or a name on it?**
> ➤ **Who needs value added services?**
> ➤ **Who should design them?**

The list of questions could become rather endless.

Where there is no vision, people perish.

-Proverbs 29:18

The same holds true for companies. In my opinion, we have always provided value added services without labeling them. To many of us, knowing what the customer needs is part of common sense. Our business world is changing rapidly and the demands on every corporation are increasing. Many budgets are being scrutinized for optimal performance, operational cost and capital expense which can lead to restructuring or outsourcing. Additionally many corporations are undergoing a flattening of management levels and even though corporate earnings seems to reach a long awaited high, most corporations are not hiring or investing in supply chain efficiencies as much as they could.

When this occurs, the pressure to *out-source* tasks and functions previously handled in-house will increase. As a matter of fact the out-sourcing of third party logistics services has indeed become one of the fastest growing segments in our industry. Outsourcing is currently taking on a new level with Cloud Computing services and SaaS where the systems possibilities and choices to outsource or change have increased dramatically. We as logistics providers; must be ready to change with our customers and quite often provide services that are not at all what are labeled as "supply chain services". Maybe it *IS* time to call services created under these conditions, value added services. Those services and system features that are out of the ordinary requiring us to create something new are the new value add. Take the never ending issue of more visibility in the supply chain, how can this be achieved?

Quite often the solution lies in technology, but most technology is very expensive and time consuming to install so what is the best solution?

We may need to forge new relationships with technology partners to provide more value add services since newer technology is driving more change. Are technical alliances with technology companies a must as we evolve into the future? Possibly, but it still comes back to the same question, Listen to what your customer wants and work together to find the solution. A combination of improved service levels and technology may be the answer. Sometimes, the fact that you can create more visibility for your customer into an area where you have always performed well will be sufficient. The fact that you now can show the customer how the task is performed and measured for successful execution, may give you many endorsements as a service provider.

Now, who said it would be easy to create and even identify any potential and new value added feature.

The answer still lies in three simple words, LISTEN, LISTEN and LISTEN.

To listen is imperative, but unless you ACT upon the information, what good will it be to you? Please re-read the three simple words above, they mean a lot to you as a sales executive. They are synonymous with success (Listen).

I think that one of the hardest tasks, once you have created a value added service, is to make that service less expensive in comparison to your customer handling this function on their own. Not an easy task, but it can and must be done. Quite often a new customer may ask for a special service where you, as a sales executive, can relate their needs to one of your other customers. You don't have to invent something new just modify and apply what you already are providing for that customer. As a matter of fact, it now appears that you have achieved a level to where you can draw from something that is highly regarded and that is *experience*.

Client development

Developing more business opportunities with your existing clients is part of the plan to establish new value added services. This may even be the best part because they know you, your product and service.

There is a possibility they even like you, why would you not be able to sell them some more services?

The long term strategy for growth and steady progress is imperative and the business incubator process is important.

Business incubators

During, and included in the maintenance plan, an <u>internal</u> client development group should be created. I tend to call these groups business incubators. Basically, you are looking at a "brain storming" group of people put together to evaluate each customer and their growth strategies. These groups also serves to make your team members feel worthwhile and recognized. It motivates them to provide extraordinary services and encourages them to continuously improve their dealings with the customers. When your internal team feels good about an accomplished business incubator process it will reflect and create more trusting and long term relationships with your customers.

In terms of a supply chain provider, you would have to create different types of incubators, depending on if the customer is local, regional, national or even global. The larger the boundaries of your customers area of operation, the more dominant the percentage of high level executives since global experience required are often only obtained over time, thus the requirement for experienced internal team members.

Don't forget some of the very best ideas come from the "front line" people. Just listen and you will soon realize the true importance of your front line team members.

Direct guidelines must be given to each incubator to empower them to function properly. The most dominant guideline given should be to evaluate each customer and try to develop value added services that can be customized to fit a particular customer. Value added services will come from overall knowledge and information gathered from your interaction with your customer. Another important factor that is prominent in the development of value added services is in-house skill, experience and the time that you are prepared to allocate. Other sources of experience could come from your network of associates and consultants.

When a shipment has been put through the "supply chain", it will be a matter for the incubator group to find out how it was handled and what could have been done differently and better. Not only from a perspective of today's shipment, but also from a future shipping pattern. When I refer to "brain storming" I really mean; the use and implementation of imagination. Your imagination really consists of creative ideas coupled with a large number of acquired skills and tools. If you use your "imagination" and the information from the maintenance plan, your in-depth knowledge of a customer and their strategy you will be able to create NEW value added services and features that this customer could use.

This could relate to virtually any physical movement within a supply chain with optimization processes. This could be for cost, routing, inventory position, ecommerce services, not to forget the systems aspects, reporting or visibility.

This is, unfortunately, not possible for all customers, but with the ones you can achieve this, you will be assured of total commitment and a long term solid relationship.

Change, a process example

Even though the sales executive may not be the actual lead in a change process it is important to understand this procedure and be ready to share with your customers. The change could become a value added service or feature that can get you the next sale.

As you look at what the business incubator process has created, the need for implementing these changes are clear. The typical steps in the change process are to assess the need, identify strategy and prepare to implement change. The change process must be owned by your team and later be introduced to the customer.

Build the internal team; help them develop the vision to engage team member action and commitment to effect the change. Pick team members that become sponsors of change and other roles for change agents. The path of communication must be established at this time so everybody concerned are properly informed.

The measurement of certain key tasks is to be recognized so you can demonstrate improvement as you make changes.

The next step would be to implement the changes and you need to create a formal change or implementation plan. This needs to be shared and communicated with the different stakeholders so you can identify cost, readiness, risk and other assessments prior to making the change.

Once you have agreement from all stakeholders you can go ahead and implement but make certain that training and awareness to support these changes are included.

There will no doubt be anticipated and non anticipated resistance to change and you need to be ready for this aspect. The demonstration of ROI (Return On Investment) or ROO (Return On Objectives) may need to be the best way of justifying change. Be open to criticism and scrutiny. Someone may have discovered more issues that can be improved, besides you have to be clear on this aspect to sustain the change.

I worked with a manufacturing company (on the other side of the fence) to implement change and although the reasons for change was pure internal manufacturing, a good supply chain provider could have identified these aspects and suggested and potentially participated in the change process.

I had identified that a manufacturing company needed to move some of their production from the West Coast to the East Coast. After analysis of the supply chain inbound and outbound to the final customer it was clear that manufacturing needed to move. I worked to pinpoint the key business and human performance needs, including key customers and stakeholders. The real opportunity was in the transportation sector and this would impact both vendors, employees, logistics and pure transportation.

The process was justified and the internal team was developed. It started out with 4 team members and ended up with over 40. The stake holders that were impacted in this process was not only the production employees but also IT; ERP, MRP, WMS, accounting, logistics, HR, engineering (to build production lines in the new location, design process etc.). The warehouse and inventory teams had to be informed, updated and inventory locations for both raw material and finished product had to be assigned. This also involved a 3PL warehouse and external transportation.

It was indeed very complex for what on the surface seemed to be a simple change, but once you go over the requirements for the process the details will surprise you.

The savings were measured in several ways including, transportation and labor cost and accounted for millions. It has been a sustained saving for the last five years and it continuous to bring real savings to the bottom line.

They have since followed the same process for additional items and added to the savings and increased efficiencies.

This is the type of change that influences and transforms our existing paradigms under which we presently do business. The objective is to create a fundamental change that can create new platforms from where to operate.

The trust factor

Remember your customer has trust in you and your company and its services. As with reputation, it takes a long time to build a trust factor, but it will take only a moment to tear it all down. This doesn't mean that you as a supply chain sales executive, customer service or operations person, should make sure to do everything personally. The old statement, "if it has to be done right I have to do it myself," should not be the first thought on your mind.

Trust does not only come into play towards your customer it is imperative within your own company. Without the trust factor, your company will not operate at optimum levels and will sooner or later also falter in the trust towards your customers. Trust, in this sense means delegating and allowing and empowering other people with responsibilities. Please remember, you are only as "strong as your weakest link". Make certain to take the necessary steps to implement quality control with imbedded continuous improvement processes throughout the whole company. Once you as a supply chain sales executive can identify the "trust factor" of your company and relate this to your existing and new potential customers a great deal of success will be achieved. A very important part in any sales presentation is where you can illustrate a "moment of trust". Please take the time to find a situation where something went wrong and then demonstrate how it was corrected. We all know that supply chain is no different than any other type of industry, things do go wrong. Once you have found a situation that you are comfortable with, study the good points where the operations personnel did exceptionally well, where they excelled, how your system caught the issue or something else you can think of.

Once this is done relate this to the customer as an example of how they can "trust" that you will competently take care of any situation. The ability to demonstrate that we "do what ever it takes" to handle a situation right. This type of action can be used very successfully mainly to obtain new accounts (and it can also satisfy deserving associates). If you are in a position to use a customers name it will even further enhance your argument, especially, if the customer is well known. Process examples like this are immense sales arguments for inducing your potential customer to choose your services over those of the competition.

SUMMARY STATEMENT

When it comes to maintenance and retention sales, I have to caution you since it is too easy for you as a sales executive to fall into the group of maintenance sales and become somewhat lazy and delay the actual "new" sales activity in favor of a more relaxed maintenance sales effort.

Time and territory management means that you have to design your own sales promotional programs to fit your schedule. You'll have to learn to factor into your agenda time/territory management and the effort required for exploration of new and additional business opportunities.

When you explore new opportunities you have to become pro-active. I mean, that it is of the utmost importance not only to learn about new business opportunities but actually acting upon them. Only to learn and know of a customers present and future requirements just isn't enough. To ACT, really means the difference, doesn't it?

PART TWO

The Next Level

"Success is not the key to happiness. Happiness is the key to success. If you love what you are doing, you will be successful."

Albert Schweitzer

Management National and Global

Sales Management – National and Global

In a more competitive environment it becomes increasingly important for the logistics and supply chain providers to compete on a national and global level. The slogan that is commonly used in the media is "globalization." This is indicative of how many top executives see their corporations and their own natural path of growth. The question that faces us most is; if we are not already, how do we become and maintain a competitive position as a "global contender?"

In the supply chain industry, we have indeed been global for many years already, just look at some of the big 3PL's such as Panalpina, Kuehne and Nagel or DB Schenker. They have grown rapidly, and in my opinion, commonly as a result of their customer requirements for expansion. If you couple that with an opportunity to create joint ventures, or simply buy a local 3PL, your chances for success increase drastically. Even pure play warehouse and distribution companies that used to be domestic are indeed "going global". Many full service logistics and supply chain (3PL's) as well as 4PL's like a CH Robinson along with FedEx and UPS are well underway with an aggressive global expansion strategy. Most supply chain providers have an aspiration of a global presence and are positioning themselves with an agency relationship or other marketable associations and affiliations. Many ocean freight carriers are promoting themselves as global carriers where the utilization of one carrier, and their equipment and infrastructure can provide synergy's that will produce a significant overall saving. Container management, by itself, is regarded as one of those benefits. Just take a look at how they manage to interchange containers between carriers – usually not an easy collaboration and not a good customer experience. Many of the ocean freight carriers have extended their service reach and are now involved in providing services in an extended supply chain beyond their original reach. Expansive collaborate partnerships with existing global 3PL's have in some cases been the path for growth.

This brings us to the issue of how your customers can expand into new countries and globalize their trade by using the services of a 3PL. Many companies are building up their capital reserves and are hesitant to spending capital. At times they prefer to create global expansion by outsourcing every activity that is not part of their core business.

➤ The pressures to out-source are intensifying, and when you add the prospect of a capital expense for facilities versus a transactional process expense it becomes evident that an outside provider of selected services is a viable alternative.

➤ This is where a supply chain – 3PL provider has to position themselves to capture the attention of top management executives who make these kind of decisions.

As the supply chain, logistics providers, we must be there to provide creative support services. We must make it easy, more of a risk free and economical solution for a customer to take that next step towards "globalization" or simply to expand to a new area of the country. For this, you will in many cases, need a national or a global account sales executive.

How do you select or develop a Global or National accounts executive?

The most common factor to look for is a long, successful career in field sales of approximately ten to twenty years. Other key skills that are required in the industry are knowledge of the total supply chain. This person should have some recognition because you would want this individual to be well known or at least have good knowledge of accounts that you will nominate under your global sales program. He has to be an excellent team player, because  national and global sales will include a large number of customer sales executives as well as accountants and other operational personnel. He has to be able to co-ordinate all functions; select services that have to be provided and negotiate the fees for such services. He needs to have extremely well developed skills for complex sales presentations. He has to be one of the best listeners; to realize, identify and interact with the different levels and departments of your customers and their companies. Many global 3PL's have additionally taken the step to create Global Teams, with account managers that are empowered to reach out to virtually all areas of a company in order to attract a customer. This is further designed to keep customers from looking elsewhere with the competition and ensuring that they can provide just about any service via in house resources. These are some of the guidelines which indicate how a global logistics expert or national sales manager could compose the proper team for each potential new national or global customer.

Experience

I was personally the key national sales director for a large warehousing corporation in Canada when a global manufacturer of cookies and crackers decided to enter the Canadian market. They considered tax ramifications, liabilities, risks, capital outlays, infrastructure and a myriad of internal issues that would deplete their internal resources. They very quickly identified that to own an operation of their own was not financially or otherwise viable as a start up mode. They, therefore, decided to out-source their warehousing and distribution requirements. I was eventually selected as the supply chain provider for these services. I was responsible to assemble and, in some cases, create all services required. During this process, I met with at least twenty different executives from this company. They were positioned in virtually all departments and their purpose was to identify every level of their requirements for each product to reach the end consumer. To answer all their questions, I accumulated a team that consisted of our accountants, operations personnel, from General Manager to warehouse managers, customs specialist, banking personnel as well as an IS team to integrate their system and make it functional in this new market. It took over six months before they were set up within this system and able to interact on all levels with their own company. Even their sales agents in Canada had to be interacted before this was to be considered a successful venture.

Without a good team, within my own organization, it would not have been possible to obtain and maintain this account. These are some of the reasons why it is so important to select the right person for global and national sales activities.

As a Global Sales Executive you must have some understanding of foreign markets and the basic "rules". In most countries a first name basis is normal; however in many European countries such as Germany, the last name is a widespread way of conducting business.

Once you have confirmed a first name basis with a German customer you have really achieved a higher level of trust as well as a certain degree of a personal relationship.

There is a dissimilarity in mentality between many European countries and even though their geographic proximity is close to each other, just crossing over that border to the next country is a world of difference. The same applies to many other global markets. To be truly successful when selling abroad you must take the time to study their environment and their cultures.

Commonly it is not enough to just study these scenarios, you can only understand the sometimes subtle difference by living in those countries. However, study this aspect is important since your effort will be noticed and could still make the difference in making a sale.

Here are some fundamental points from which a national or global accounts sales strategy could be formed and identified:

> You have to identify and make certain that your own infrastructure and existing services and offices are prepared to take on global and national accounts with more demanding service requirements.

> Strengths and weaknesses within your own company.

> What are the required additional investment in infrastructure, personnel, and systems?

➢ Increased sales activity?

➢ Re-training of sales personnel with new sales techniques and probing questions?

➢ Development of new marketing strategies.

➢ New power point presentations and brochures with a new type of presentation format.

➢ Possible change of company image? Selection of value added services (does a national or global account need different value added services)?

➢ Relationship between your offices, inclusive of profit sharing.

➢ Market activity.

➢ Competitors.

  ➢ Know who they are their strengths and weaknesses

➢ Branding and marketing of the new program.

➢ How to measure success with this program.

➢ The time and cost factor of creating a global and national accounts program.

➢ Should you target specific markets and countries?

➢ Selection of additional partners, services or discontinuance of relationships.

➢ How to provide focus and leadership for the rest of the organization?

When selecting possible target accounts you have to identify:

- ➢ existing customers.
- ➢ new customers.
- ➢ multinational corporations.
- ➢ existing markets.
- ➢ new markets.
- ➢ existing services.
- ➢ market intelligence, how to obtain and feed back within your own company.

There are several more items which have to be considered when starting out on a global and national sales campaign however, one of the most important issues for success is the actual training of your local sales executives. Without the training, and the day to day support from your front line sales executives, most sincere efforts for such a program will fail.

You will also need to provide some training and information to your day to day operations personnel in order for them to be able to identify a potential global or national accounts opportunity. I could be as bold as to say, that if you are attempting to start a global, national accounts sales program, make sure that the idea, concept and every nuance of this program is well sold within your own company first. I have seen many good and viable sales programs fail and fall into obscurity, just because the support was not obtained from within the company.

Sometimes the issue of change is the hardest part to sell internally since we have always done it this way and we are still profitable. However if you do not evolve with the market you will sooner or later end up as a losing proposition.

- **As I have said before, you are only as strong as your weakest link.**

Do we really need sales training?

Being a "natural" sales executive is no longer sufficient to become successful. The skill level that is required in our industry is rapidly increasing and regardless of your "natural" abilities you will without a doubt require some degree of serious and professional training. No one in the logistics industry can afford to have a poorly trained or informed sales executive in the field. Such a reflection on your company quickly becomes a real detriment to an otherwise well deserved reputation.

Some pointers to refresh our sales activities:

Stop procrastinating...

Have you heard this before, but never done anything about it. Maybe you have said, well as of next week I will change this or that. Please re-read the text above and change at least one thing immediately. You have to start making those changes or prepare that sales quotation or whatever "that" task is. Think in terms of now.

Tomorrow, next week, later and similar words are correlated to failure as is the word never.

Plan sales calls...

I firstly recommend to research the customer you intend to see and focus on the outcome of selling a specific service. Secondly, identify (before your visit) exactly what you want to sell or introduce. For example, if you have a LCL service to the West Coast of USA, via a mini land bridge to the east coast, make certain that you can introduce this product efficiently. When you can confirm that this is a tested and proven service with a great performance a customer is more likely to accept the proposal.

The sales pitch...

It cannot be said enough, that the planning of a sales call serves the purpose of creating a "sales pitch." I recommend practicing this sales pitch, word by word until it is perfect and can be delivered within one minute. Make sure the benefit statement is included.

Make appointments...

In order to get a solid performance with a steady success, you will have to make appointments. It is indeed important to do what is referred to as "drop in calls," however, a mix of both is imperative. The majority of calls must be on an appointment basis since most of the real decision makers are far too busy not to plan their days carefully.

Try to concentrate your appointments in a specific area during a day or week to reduce travel time and expenses. This should apply even if you do not have an out of town trip scheduled.

Make a short list and indicate items that you have or have not accomplished or completed. When you have to make a follow up appointment to present a quotation or to simply make that telephone call, do not to procrastinate this particular aspect of your sales activities. A correct, professional follow up is another key to constant success in supply chain and logistics sales.

Some thoughts on the training process

When a new sales person is selected, it is firstly imperative that the company has a good selection process. This process must ensure that a high quality new employee (or one for re-training to sales) is selected. Realistically it does not make any sense to train someone that can't adapt to sales reasonably quick, it's too costly. As a sales person, you must have a good degree of motivation and a sincere desire to succeed. As a sales manager or the sales trainer each training process should be re-enforced and a suitable number of repetitions and practices should be undertaken. Other areas of training have to be targeted on NON selling activities. Make sure that the sales person understands and recognizes the need for NON selling activities but make sure that it is identified and understood how much of these types of activities are actually required and how long they should take. It is quite common to consider the 9-5 time as selling time and dedicate additional overtime to NON selling activities but does that make sense?

Of course not, we have to balance our days and our time in such as fashion that all aspects and tasks have adequate time allocation.

One other important part of sales training is to react and respond to customer inquiries. Did you know that in an overall study (product oriented) over 40% of all inquiries were responded to too late to be of any use to the potential customer! Although this is a strong indicator of a dangerous trend in sales, the nature of our business is actually demanding a much more prompt response to a customer inquiry. Regardless, it is worth noting that even the "high paced" supply chain industry has a few instances of non-response and late responses. After all we're not completely perfect.

Which format is most beneficial in sales training?

Traditionally there is <u>group training</u> and <u>individual training</u>. Each category is split into information based and participation training.

Information based

Typical information based training would be lectures for a group. Other information based training would be manuals and bulletins designed to target each individual. There are a number of sales consultancy companies that provide a variety of sales programs that can indeed be very helpful. Most of these companies do not have a specific supply chain sales training course. These methods are essential and have to be balanced to ensure proper penetration and absorption of fundamental information by each sales executive.

Participation training

The participation training is more difficult to undertake or undergo. Many of us feel uncomfortable in group discussions or role playing. Other formats are simulation panels with questions and answers, the objective is to have each sales person take an active part in the training and this is one way of doing so. Many sales trainers also suggest the "VIDEO training" method. This would put a sales executive in front of a group to perform a sales presentation. This whole presentation would then be video taped and later played back to the group for evaluation and comments. This would then be repeated several times and the improvement would be noted. The video would eventually be given to each sales executive to play in their own privacy.

Participation and Individual

A more costly but sometimes more effective way of participation training is individual training. This would entail:

> **On the job training.**
> **Personal conferences.**
> **Individual instruction.**
> **Job rotation between departments.**
> **Sales calls together with a senior sales person.**

Individual evaluation of such activities and constructive praise and criticism could prove to be much more beneficial than any other form of group training.

I recommend developing a personalized training system with a "one on one" format. Ultimately, this will provide rapid quality results, and the sooner a sales person is well trained the sooner significant results can be expected. I am not saying that this is an inexpensive way of training, it should be recognized this is a considerably more expensive exercise.

Provided the initial selection process of a sales person is properly developed the end results will be well worth the extra effort and cost.

The presentation

We have all seen some terrible presentations and proposals and a fewer number of really high quality proposals. The scope of a proposal often dictates the quantity and sometimes the quality of the content suffers. I firmly believe the bar has been raised significantly in our industry and there is no excuse for us not to have a professional presentation in all aspects.

Does it come down to price and not service?

It's true that many 3PL's, 4PL's, freight forwarders and other logistics providers basically can offer the same level of service so logically it would be a price question? For this reason it has become more evident and increasingly important to differentiate your company's infrastructure, management depth and the services offered.

Major tools when differentiating your services has to be with websites, proposals, presentations and brochures. When a customer has requested proposals from a number of logistics providers yours must be outstanding!

If your presentation looks better, but essentially contains the same information and services as your competitors, it is quite common that emotions will rule in the final decision. The logistics provider could be chosen because of presentation format.

Brochures

Please take a moment to evaluate your present brochure and its overall presentation format including all of your power point presentations. How elaborate should you make your brochure? Think of what it will be designed to do. Should it inform your customer at the first meeting of all your services and benefits, or should it be a brochure that creates interest for you to return with a complete proposal?

Is it designed to be used with cold call sales? Here are some questions that should be considered when the deciding on which type of brochure to use:

> Should it be inexpensive enough that you can accept a large number of potential clients will simply throw it away or ignore it?

> Should you create an expensive brochure where you hope the customer will not throw it away because it is expensive and because it contains valuable information?

> Should you create one brochure of each to allow your reps to leave which ever brochure they see fit or simply email as follow up?

> Should you have no brochure at all and simply rely on a Power Point generated proposal?

> Should you combine all of the above?

Is a customer personalized/customized proposal or brochure your most important goal?

How do you differentiate yourself in your promotional literature and presentations?

> Define your product and the service you provide. Then decide on your focus and target group. This group could be geographical or product oriented i.e., computer companies for an air freight forwarder.

> List your alternative services, slogans and special features of your services. Define which of your services will be the easiest to sell.

Identify which service will provide the largest return and become the most profitable and let this be the main focus of the brochure. Once you have some of these items on a piece of paper, eliminate services that won't work, or services that are of lesser quality and make less money (be honest in your evaluation). Find out what the competition is offering. It is OK to "steal" ideas to improve on something that your competition obviously did or did not do well. Watch out for copyrights, trademarks and registered use or infringements.

Keep in mind you have only approximately 20 seconds to get the attention of a busy executive. If your brochure doesn't create enough interest within this time frame chances are your brochure was poorly made and will be ineffective. Let's look at how to get a potential customer to see your professional presentation.

> **The cold call**. What do you leave your potential customer during or after the initial meeting? Using your well rehearsed sales pitch, do you give a brochure, or can you confirm that you will return with a proposal and don't leave anything? Obviously, there is no simple answer to this question but rather several solutions. The optimal way, in my opinion, is to leave your business card, a brief brochure and have an agreement to return with a proposal.

> **The presentation.** At this time it is important to have a quality presentation with material of high standards which will give a professional impression and is up to date. Explaining that a certain service just seized to exist or a new

one is just not in your brochure yet are two safe ways of losing credibility.

> ## The Personalized Power Point Presentation

Since I have created a number of these let me share some ideas that you could consider when preparing your own presentation:

> Give some consideration to how you will layout the proposal.

> Create a printed

"binder" and make sure it is professional.

The actual layout of the presentation can and should, in most cases, start with a customized "Executive Statement" addressing the main area of request pertaining to the reason you are submitting the presentation. If you have not identified your real objective or how you intend to provide logistics services, you can, briefly outline your intentions, other associated services and other amenities. I strongly recommend creating a few chapters that always are "standard" and automatically enclosed regardless of why or who you provide this proposal to.

They could include:

- ➢ Company profile and history
- ➢ Quality statements, ISO, lean certifications
- ➢ Office locations, domestic and/or international and maps
- ➢ Outline of all services provided and an introduction of personnel, departments and the different services available.
- ➢ Agency agreements
- ➢ Trade references
- ➢ Information systems, IT set up.
- ➢ Financial information; Annual report or excerpts.
- ➢ Service Awards and complimentary letters from your customers (these are very good marketing tools and should be used as often as possible).
- ➢ Published Web Statements or Newspaper or other types of publications including what you can find on the web.
- ➢ Special licenses; customs brokerage license, NVOCC
- ➢ Terms and conditions under which you do business (this is an area that is often omitted but should be enclosed. This refers the transportation terms as well. If you decide not

to include this make sure you reference these terms and conditions. Especially point out any liability issues in the event of loss or damages).

Other customized chapters could be:

> Export and Import services.
> Brokerage services.
> Domestic services.
> FCL, LCL and container management.
> Consolidated services and service lanes or service areas.
> Consulting services.
> Value added services.
> Insurance services.
> Information systems, IT Platforms, System Integration tools, EDI, capabilities, system and supply chain visibility.
> Payment terms and conditions, invoicing. procedures and summary invoicing
> Currency applications.
> Rates/pricing schedules.
> Published articles relating to the issues at hand.
> Marketing and trend statements.

Most proposals do not contain a synopsis; however, I
find this to be a very good addition because it will
give you an opportunity to once more deliver your
strongest point.

This list can be improved and expanded upon;
however, it will assist you in developing or improving
your presentation.

Power Point formats of personalized presentations are very common.
This is why it is imperative to differentiate your proposal. It is the
main reason why you have to spend <u>more time,</u> <u>effort</u> and <u>money</u> in
the initial stages of creating a great <u>presentation</u>.

Interactive presentations

The next generation of presentations is obviously the online
interactive presentations. The scenarios of "what if" situation with
changing variables becomes extremely effective with this type of
visual delivery. These presentations can more or less, contain
similar information, but can have the added benefit of movement
within graphics or other areas. They can provide a "what if" feature.
This can be one of your most impressive sales tools, provided you
have the time and the attention of your prospect or audience. You
can differentiate your company significantly by introducing a "live"
proposal with the "what if" feature, but you must be absolutely

certain that your system is 100% operational. Many of the 3PL's and Global Providers have live tracking systems and a live presentation that enables the customer additional visibility in "real time" is indeed a powerful tool. The reporting tools and report writers can be very effectively presented in a live format where you can sort and use live data.

Once you add PO (Purchase Order) Management and other features, you can get ahead of some of your competition,.

If the presentation is not working right, you lose not only the benefit point but also creditability and trust. Losing the trust from a potential customer over a system can be devastating.

On the other hand the system may function but I'm not the only person who has seen a presentation where it became quite evident that the presenter was not well prepared. Often it was clear the sales executive was simply not familiar enough with this type of presentation or the function of the computer software or system. These types of excuses made under these circumstances are to be avoided at all costs. Even though your computer system may be very operational and everything is working normally, any doubt of your ability to operate your computer during a presentation can have future doubts in the customer's mind. This will most certainly reduce your chances of obtaining his business.

When you are making a presentation based on an online or other software presentation, the risk is significant that your presentation could become impersonal. Don't forget that this is still a people business and one of the most important factors in any successful sale is you, the sales person.

Closing questions

Don't forget those closing questions such as:

- **What is the most important factor for you to select our services?**

- **When would it be an opportune time to start using our services?**

You should obviously not forget to ask questions throughout the presentation where you could use questions such as:

- **What do you like about this part of our service?**

- **What is the one thing you need improved upon considering your current provider?**

- **Why would this be a deciding factor to you?**

- **How do you propose we design this service?**

- **Is there any aspect of our service where we could further improve and customize for you?**

Know all your questions, practice them and ask them diligently, the answers will create more sales opportunities.

Advertising and Press releases

Besides of sending out emails, brochures etc., don't underestimate the power of the press and send out as many press releases as you possibly can. Remember, the items used must be newsworthy and not simply advertising (although it most commonly is). Advertising is mostly in trade magazines and via websites and SEO or pay per click web applications.

What about "Give-a-ways" and Gifts?

I am of the opinion that give-a-ways should be sparingly used (maybe I am just cheap...). It is quite often a corporate rule of your customer <u>not</u> to accept any gifts what so ever. This particularly refers to the more

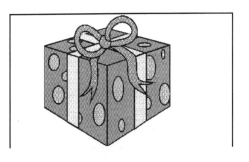

elaborate and expensive gifts. The "traditional" Christmas present is in many business communities are virtually abolished and frequently misconstrued as one form or another of "bribery". The functional gifts such as reasonably good pens and pads with your logo and other relevant information appear to be more readily accepted in the business community. At least most pens and pads will not be considered a bribe. Let me give you an example of how I once used an inexpensive pen to obtain a new account:

This was my second meeting, I had already obtained the information and was returning with a proposal. The logistics issue was air freight from the Far East. I presented my proposal in detail and made sure that all details and rates were fully explained and understood by the client. I asked a leading question pertaining to what would it really take for him to switch his traffic over to my company. I elaborated on price versus service and transit time. He was evasive and responded that a complete evaluation had to be done prior to any commitment. At this particular moment, he happened to notice my pen with our company's logo. It was actually the one I was using and I had no intentions of giving it away. He said, "Does that pen write well?" "Yes it does," was my reply, and then he asked, "Can I try it?" I still didn't want to give my only pen away but responded, "Would you like to have it?" He said, "Only if it writes well." Fortunately, it did and he made the statement that he would like to keep it if all right with me. At this point, what can you do?

I would have to go and buy another pen for the rest of the day which would be an inconvenience to me so, I simply said, "If you want the pen you'll have to give me a few shipments." He looked at me in bewilderment and said, "I can't give you a shipment right away, you know I have to study your proposal."

I said, "No problem, I understand that you can't give me a shipment today," and then I added, "Tomorrow would be just fine." He started to laugh and the conversation went to a very friendly level. He promised to study this proposal right away and let me know. I always referred to the pen, each time I spoke with him. Even after he became a good customer I always made sure to have a new pen when I went to see him.

This will have a lasting impression on your customer by remembering these types of details and using them to your benefit. I still recommend using give-a-ways sparingly however making sure the item you choose is of an inexpensive, but a quality kind product because it can be an excellent promotional tool.

Rejection, is it personal?

You made your presentation and the potential customer refuses to use your services, NOW WHAT?

Rejection is possibly the hardest part of being a sales executive although it is most commonly <u>not</u> personal but more directed towards your company, How do you effectively deal with it? Can there be a universal answer to this question? I don't think so. Let's face it as individuals we take criticism very differently, not to mention direct rejection is the hardest to take.

One good strategy is to agree with what your potential customer says, at least as a beginning. This will give you some time to ask some more questions and tactfully later disagree and to establish if this is the only and true objection.

Analysis of rejection

My recommendation is to always take one "step" away from the sales call, analyze what was said, and try to find out where the real objections were or what were the reasons behind the final rejection. Sometimes it is evident why the potential customer decided against using your services, but quite often it's more complex than that, consider was it

1. price
2. service (or lack of service)
3. reputation
4. presentation
5. associated costs
6. personnel
7. infrastructure or office locations
8. system set up and interconnectivity
9. lack of value added services
10. present service
11. bond with an existing supplier of supply chain services
12. is the time not right, is it seasonally impractical due to peak volumes
13. is it simply a matter of more information is required
14. or what?

Could it be more on a monetary level in regards to line of credit or payment terms? Is their company in poor financial health, not enough allocated in the budget? Maybe you were not speaking with the real decision maker and your efforts are just being stopped before they attract attention from the real decision maker. This action by a non-decision making individual is actually more common than most of us think. It could be that this person is protecting the territory for one reason or another. You'll have to feel some sort of comfort level to go over their head to the next person or the real decision maker. Going over someone's head may not be the ultimate solution instead you may have to enter into the process of selling to multiple decision makers. To ask for other team members that would be interested and see if a meeting could be arranged is a good way to approach this. At that time you would go over your presentation again.

As you can see this list can indeed be endless. Regardless it serves the purpose well to analyze and try to establish why you were unsuccessful in obtaining this business. It is good for your own mental health's sake and it will give you an indication as to what you have to change to obtain this account on your next visit. It will also provide you with useful information that you can apply when you meet your next customer of this nature and similar set of circumstances. Some people even call this "experience"...

I am not discouraged, because every wrong attempt discarded is another step forward - Thomas Edison

Price objection

In this competitive environment of supply chain, logistics sales, it is quite common that price is the real objection. Try to go around the issue, for example say, "If I could show you that our price is more than fair and our service is worth every dime you'd pay, would you switch over to us?"

This is a real give away, because if your customer has said, no I will not switch to you, obviously price is NOT the issue. This will give you an opportunity to ask more leading questions and try to get to the root of the problem of what  were the actual reasons for the rejection. Quite often a direct question requesting him to identify the real problem will get the proper answer. It is most certainly worth the time to ask this question.

If the price is the real objection, try to find out what is included in your competitors price. For example, if you are selling air freight, is the pick up or delivery included, handling fees, customs clearance, etc. If you are dealing in warehousing and distribution, maybe the fees for in and out handling are included in your competitors bid and not yours, or maybe they offer some free storage time. The customer may be thinking, "Why should I pay more?" Here are some good reasons why a customer might consider paying a little more:

- Experience/Personnel
- Stability of the company
- Better service and facilities
- Higher frequency
- More flexibility
- A variety of value added service
- Possible customization of services or personalized service or more service alternatives
- Hours of availability
- Emergency and contingency plans / back up services
- Computer capabilities the company's' network, associated companies
- Full service logistics provider
- Owned vehicles
- Availability of equipment i.e. containers, trucks etc.
- Insurance, credit terms, line of credit, or OEM capabilities
- Distribution locations, capabilities, pick and pack etc.
- Ecommerce integrated fulfillment
- Delivery infrastructure, FTL, LTL, FedEx, UPS, USPS
- Rate optimization engines for TL/LTL and small parcel

There are many more positive suggestions you can make to persuade the customer to use your services. Always try to demonstrate that it is justifiable to spend a little more for that extra service and/or quality your company provides. After all, the success of the customer's company depends on their choice of a good supply chain provider. Do not fail to sell the concept of service.

What if the supply chain service did fail? What is the worse case scenario? Is it not safer to pay a little more for extra quality and additional service? I think so.

- Sell value and benefit over price as often as you can.

Remember you must establish a high level of confidence in you as a sales person and a high level of confidence in your company and its services, without this the sales process will either fail or be extended until you can ascertain this condition.

LISTEN, LISTEN and LISTEN hear what your client is saying not just what he says.

When these types of objections come up always try to answer in a way that resolves the issue. I'm trying to illustrate that if the price is too low and your competitors are charging less than what you are proposing they are possibly NOT making enough money to sustain top service over the long haul. Most purchasers of a supply chain service realize this. I have quite often heard, "I don't know how they make any money on our shipments." The common law of business balances on paying a little and getting a lot simply cannot be done. Because of the existing business environment, many shippers and supply chain purchasers still maintain the "cheaper way" (although they know better) and you simply cannot obtain the business with a more expensive rate. There are, however, other factors that would dictate low cost transportation only, such as the financial situation of the company who is seeking a low cost transporter or the actual costing/profit margins of the product. These types of factors would typically dictate that the price **is** the only criteria for a choice of a logistics service and mode of transportation.

Every time you are successful in overcoming an objection, confirm this fact back to the customer to make continuous agreements as the sales call progresses.

If you still are not successful in overcoming the objection, you could use as a customer reference letter/email or even better if you have someone that can be contacted for a reference.

If you still cannot get any closer to obtaining the account, my advice would be to schedule a strategic long term plan of attack and keep coming back to this account. Try building a relationship and if possible a friendship. One day your opportunity will come. The time will arise when it becomes a matter of being on the "rescue list" when something does go wrong and it inevitably will. Many of us give up too quickly on a potential account. Please don't forget that many of your potential customer's needs are always changing.

Their selected logistics provider may not always be the best choice for their new requirements. When you are on their list as a potential logistics provider your opportunity could come. This is a classic example of why it is imperative that you give your potential client a comprehensive presentation of what your company can do and what services you offer. The long or short term strategy for closing an account is most times ignored, although, this strategy should be addressed first. It is imperative to schedule this type of strategy into your sales activity, since many accounts are simply not obtained because you forgot to call back. On the other side of the coin, you may have not have called often enough during a short period of time, and strategy is even more important when you are trying to obtain a national account or a multinational account.

Some pointers for simple strategic planning;

> **Analyze** your current service in relation to the customer's requirements and objectives.
> **Evaluate** alternative services, that have or should be invented, altered or changed.
> **Create** an action plan. Test the plan (this can be done with your own management, sales meetings, other clients, this client etc).
> Decide what could have been done better, then **revise** the plan.
> Look for feedback during the next test phase and **re-assess**.

By using this cycle in the strategic decision making process, you will realize a "formula" that will meet your own objectives. It may not be the solution for all your clients but it will give you the base and general direction.

As mentioned with a professional presentation and good salesmanship, a customized proposal of your services can be suited to fit a larger number of clients. Always keep in mind whether this proposal can be realistically attainable and presentable, and what you have to change in this presentation to obtain this particular account? Is the proposal clear, has a concise offer and does it focus on a specific outcome? Does it meet the customer priorities, constraints and business objectives? Did you use the correct language and style for this target audience? Does it outline the appropriate features, benefits and advantages?

Ask yourself these questions and be honest in your response, not forgetting to listen to that "gut feeling."

Would I do business with me?

This phrase has been used by many sales trainers (including me) and it is a very important question, well worth repeating. Again, an honest answer could save you from wasting a lot of time and increase your chance of being successful.

To have a clear "base strategy" will be essential to having a steady successful path. This path to success is typically predictable and can be illustrated by levels of achievement.

The law of average is the more times you try the more likely you will succeed. After you have had a success streak you have reached a certain plateau. After this time, you tend to "level off" and to take it a little bit easier and a slight decline in performance usually happens.

We usually like to sit back and analyze how successful we have been. It is quite normal for any sales person to reach a plateau and this should be recognized by a good sales trainer and manager.

The need for appropriate praise will help the successful salesman to excel again and to succeed through the process towards the next plateau. At this point, we all feel a lot better about ourselves and

confidence is gained as well as useful experience. To realize this and actually reach a new plateau, somewhat higher than the previous one, provides for a healthy trend towards growth.

This is where the process starts all over again until we reach yet the next plateau.

The real key to enhancing your skills and rate of success is to learn to enjoy and appreciate each plateau just as much as the upward surges. Your leaps will become bigger and your "staying power" is on a positive avenue that will ultimately bring you to a secure path for future success.

How to sell to the manufacturer or CPG

How do you convince a manufacturer that your services are what they require?

How do you illustrate the benefits of using your company in relation to services and overall cost reduction?

One of the most difficult tasks is to understand exactly what a manufacturer requires to facilitate his OEM supply as well as other items imported for direct sales or production activities. Let's assume that you are indeed a "global logistics supplier" that is capable of providing a service from raw material to end consumer. I realize that some of these areas may be specialized and your individual situation and/or services may only apply to one or more segments of the supply chain. I would like to point out, that regardless of your firms possible segmented interaction with each manufacturer, your personal understanding of the total supply chain requirements could be paramount to you in obtaining any of their supply chain business. This is applicable, regardless, if you are selling inland trucking, air freight, JIT services or ocean freight. Your chances for success increase with your personal enhanced knowledge, ability to understand and identify the logistics and the end to end supply chain.

To become successful in selling to a manufacturing company who imports their raw material and/or parts for manufacturing and exporting of a finished product, you have no choice but to try to understand their total process. This means from conceptual sourcing stage through total life cycle of product to delivered the final end recipient. There is an aspect I like to refer to as the "Ripple effect" and that means you have to understand what changes in one area of the company will do to another area where the "Ripple effect" may be felt.

What levels and departments do you interact with?

Let us assume that this is a company that imports parts for the manufacturing process from the Far East. They manufacture a product "Made in the USA" and export to other world markets. Your first step should be, in most cases, to interact with the appointed supply chain/traffic and/or distribution manager/director/VP. You have to understand their areas of influence and responsibility before you can actively proceed to other departments within the manufacturing company. I have always found it to be a good idea to obtain the appointed managers approval to ask further questions on how to understand for example the purchasing process. Interaction with the purchasing departments is essential to comprehend the complete requirements of any manufacturing company.

Try asking any purchasing agent or manager if they can accurately predict their requirements for next season. Without a doubt, they will all say their requirements and forecasts change several times throughout the season.

For example, the R&D department could decide that a design change for any part of the final product is required or the Quality department could find that a certain part suddenly does not meet specified criteria. It could be something as "simple" as the production quality does not meet the standards or specifications of the sample. There could be a myriad of reasons. Regardless, this will prompt the purchasing department to react to find a new item or have a modification made of an existing item. Because of this change of new items, the supply chain requirements will change. The new part will be needed for the same production cycle; however it will only be available at a much later date. This would imply the need for air freight; hopefully the purchasing department will call on the traffic department to analyze the requirements and identify the changes. By being pro-active, you can readily establish a relationship with both the purchasing and traffic departments and combine your sales effort by arranging meetings with both departments simultaneously. I have already mentioned the concept of creating "*golden handcuffs*" on your clients and this is one way of ensuring that the cuffs don't come off. You should become the only logical choice for logistics and supply chain services in any situation.

If there is a requirement change from ocean freight to air freight they should have the confidence in your capability to call you first. If they feel you comprehend their total logistics practices and needs they will feel comfortable in the fact that you do understand your part of this chain and how important your performance and services are in relation to the end result.

How do they really think?

The purchasing/procurement department that is... Because they had to change the mode of transportation from ocean to air freight the cost has changed. The purchasing agent will typically (this is simplified of course) go to the purchasing manager or vice president and outline the additional cost per item. Since the increased cost per individual item could be significant, directly because the mode of transportation has changed, you as the logistics provider must have "educated" the purchasing agent of your variety of choices. As their appointed logistics provider you should strive to understand the cost increases and suggest alternative ways of reducing the actual landed transportation costs. Quite often the purchasing department has been told by the manufacturing department that the parts are required by a certain date. By asking the right questions, including purchasing terms, you can determine the required quantities and possibly suggest a mix of transportation services to meet the production lines time frame. Suggest that the first part be flown, but the second part can be sent via ocean freight. In these incidences the finance department becomes very important as well and to have connections in this area will never hurt you.

They will typically order via their ERP software, internet or use some e-Procurement tools such as Ariba or Basware or even work through a procurement service. The total process is very rapid so if you are not tied into this you can easily be bypassed to provide transportation and other services. The purchasing terms may also dictate FOB factory which can mean you are not involved in this transaction at all.

A pro-active stance with your clients will render you the advantage of being "one step ahead" and always considered the only choice as their logistics and supply chain provider.

Try to understand the inventory management process, lead time and what criteria is applied to maintain adequate inventory levels. Ask what variables are considered to ensure that sufficient parts and raw materials are in the supply chain to comply with the manufacturing process. Maybe you have to meet with the inventory manager to see how they relate to the purchasing department. Or maybe you even have an opportunity to provide warehousing services. They usually work very close with each other, and by having a relationship with each department you will become their extended department or even the link between the different departments. The purchasing process is a large chapter in itself and to understand the total process in this respect requires a lot of in depth analysis of each manufacturer. As a supply chain provider, you have a responsibility to establish a relationship with the purchasing department and ensure they know exactly what kind of services you are capable of providing. If you can establish a closer relationship and be known as the "go to" person when a crisis develops, you have come a long way.

I was working for an international freight forwarder, and one of my clients with whom I had a very good relationship, called me. He had just been informed by his quality department that one of the parts for a hand held electrical tool was not performing as promised. There was an issue of returning some defective parts and the associated application for duty drawback and credit. The more critical issue was to set up proficient transportation to move the new parts to the manufacturing plant on time for the revised production time. Because of my open relationship with the purchasing department, I could co-ordinate my scheduling with their traffic department and analyze the real time need. I also met with the inventory manager as well as the quality manager to discuss their requirements. Based on these discussions I developed a pro-active "Just In Time" system and we managed to "feed" the production line as the parts became available.

This illustrates the fact that my interaction with the several departments within this manufacturing company enabled me to define the real time requirements for both my client as well as identification of most appropriate means of transportation. If I would not have had the timely interaction with all departments it is possible, I would have been called only when the traffic manager was made aware of the serious situation. At this stage, there would have been no other alternative but to provide a "last minute" panic shipment pattern. During a last minute shipment scenario, there is always a very high degree of risk. If you ever heard of Murphy's law, this could be a good time to remember *"If something can go wrong it will go wrong."*

A "panic" shipment pattern is always very costly to your client. You, on the other hand, will most probably be under pressure to lower your costs and the issue of how to cut costs without jeopardizing the service level becomes a reality. Even if the total shipment goes without a problem, a clever competitor can always make a comment on both the service and cost factors. If you have a high degree of loyalty, you most probably have no reason for concern; however, how strong is loyalty when there is a price attached?

How to manage the manufacturer's vendors

A few years ago, this area was for most logistics providers off limits. Today, I believe, this to be one of the most vital aspects of a logistics relationship with any manufacturer. You should develop systems to measure each of their vendors' performance. You could easily follow and document issues such as: On time availability of product, packaging, quality of invoices and provide communications with the vendor on the local level. Another value added service provided by many forwarders is to perform quality inspections of merchandise prior to shipping. Indeed, this is an important area of additional services and revenues that many supply chain providers could furnish. There is also a group of companies that actually specialize in this and it may be a good idea for you to be aware of these types of value added service companies.

To create a matrix of evaluation levels where you measure the interaction with your clients vendors is a very good idea and a real example of strategic partnership with your client.

I recently met with a freight forwarding executive who explained that they are routinely advised to pick up merchandise from a number of vendors in the Far East. Your client here at home has been advised by the vendor that the merchandise will be ready at a certain time. He further added that we contact the vendor only to find out that the shipment is not ready for a number of days or even

weeks. Because there is a time difference to the Far East, real
information quite often is misplaced, missed or simply over looked.
The idea to look even deeper into the supply chain and manage the
vendors suppliers is becoming extremely important. Lead times
especially in the Far East are often not correct and only if you stay
on top of the extended supply chain can you get real information. In
the end, your client will or could blame you for not picking up the
merchandise on time. This particular executive has made his
company relate back to their clients of any deviation of the
scheduled departure thus eliminating any room for error. This is a
costly, and sometimes labor intensive task, but he claims that in the
end this type of communication really pays off handsomely. If you
have this kind of system, or are planning to develop this type of
information feedback, you as a sales executive should take an active
role and use this information when you interact with your clients.
You could, for example, take this compilation of data, assemble it
into a matrix and personally discuss your clients' vendors'
performance. This is an area that will give you a very close
relationship with your client. Naturally you have to be diplomatic in
your approach when criticizing your client or his vendors. On that
same aspect, if there is negative criticism that has to be relayed, you
should discuss with your operations who should act as the "bad guy"
and who should become the solution provider.

Who will be allowed to understand the manufacturing company?

A dumb question, but if you start thinking about why should they entrust you with their total requirements if you are not qualified to understand *their* process? This is precisely my point. I will repeat myself, we must as logistics and supply chain providers strive to, at all times, understand the <u>total</u> process. We have to become an integrated part with each of our manufacturing and other supply chain partners import and export programs. This applies even if you are awarded only a certain service segment.

Let's say you are relatively new in the field of supply chain sales, how do you obtain and receive the manufacturing company's inside information?

Listen and ask questions are part of the answer, this is typically not a quick process and some tenacity is required.

Joint Sales Calls

A joint sales call with senior or specialized colleagues from your company is a good idea. As a supply chain sales executive, you have to learn to identify when there is a need for joint sales calls. You have to accept and keep one goal in mind which is to obtain their business and to be their supply chain provider. This is not the time for individual pride, because your personal lack of knowledge may very well be the end of an attempt to obtain their business.

We have all heard of the situation where a sales executive says, "I don't know the answer to that question, but I will find out and refer back to you." This is good sense and will work under many scenarios as long as you DO call back with the information. (Of course *YOU* will call back, but many of your competitors will forget).

Today's truth is that most of supply chain management teams from the manufacturing companies has no time to wait. The competition may be more knowledgeable and can have the answers instantly. However, if you've had the foresight to bring along one of your colleagues in anticipation of questions in an area not relating to your expertise, you would have had a better chance of obtaining their business. Besides the advantage of having a specialized or a senior colleague with you to answer questions, you will learn something new that you can apply to future clients.

The picture of servicing a manufacturing company or a pure importing or exporting company is becoming more complex. You have to apply many more resources to reach all levels and departments within these companies, For example, it may be wise to have your customs brokerage manager join you on sales visits to the purchasing manager. There are undoubtedly many areas where the application of tariffs could significantly reduce the landed cost and only a customs broker could provide enough information to adequately furnish an appropriate response. There may be a time when you would need the president of your company to interact with the president of the manufacturing company you are dealing with just to open up additional levels of communication.

Strategic selling on a variety of levels and departments has always made good sense. As a primary contact, you should try to develop the ability to identify when it is important to ask your superiors or colleagues to interact with you. Even though you may be on a commission, you would not be able to earn any money without the extra help of your associates. As a matter of fact, I would suggest that as soon as you have obtained the business; try to make every effort to introduce your superiors or the president of your company to their upper management. This is a very good policy and it will give you some extra *"golden handcuffs"* on several other departments if it is done right.

Key accounts

What and who are they and why should you consider a customer as a "Key Account"?

Many sales professionals have tried to establish what a real key account is and frequently the 80/20 rule is applied. "20% of my customers provides for 80% of my profits". Those 20% of customers are usually considered "key accounts." Others are more pessimistic in their outlook and claim that 10% of your sales account for 90% of your total business. Those 10% would logically be your "Key Accounts." It is, however, important to establish the "key accounts" since you would want to cut down on waste and concentrate a lot of your efforts on those 10 or 20%. Don't forget to evaluate and take into consideration if an account that has a significant potential for growth. This is obviously a type of subjective evaluation however a certain percentage of your so called "Key Accounts" should fall into this category.

Key Account Management teams are quite frequently built to seriously identify these potential accounts. Once identified, a methodical and often time consuming process is instituted to detail these key accounts real requirements. This process should encourage an interaction with these customers "key managers" to confirm all their requirements.

A SOP (Standard Operating Process) document should then confirm the exact procedure that all parties can agree upon. Your chances of maintaining such an account increases significantly once you have gone through this total process.

This once again illustrates the importance of maintenance sales which will help you with the assessment of a potential Key account.

Key accounts are natural customers that you should consider collaborating with and review their supply chains as their requirements evolve and change.

A high level of communication is necessary to maintain at <u>all</u> management levels.

PART THREE

Supply Chain sales for Ocean Freight, Truck, Warehousing, Distribution, Air Freight and Parcel

How to sell without lowering the rate
Selling Value over Price

The SCM Principle – The Supply Chain Management Principle and Collaboration with your customer

One of the most difficult issues is to know how to position the actual rates involved in any particular proposal. Is your only choice one of reducing the rates and as a result obtaining the business because you are the cheapest logistics provider?

This does happen; however, for certain commodities and a "smarter" purchaser of logistics and supply chain services rate may not always be the real problem or the reason for a change to your company.

There could be many reasons why a low rate approach is not successful. As mentioned, it could be a matter of a personal relationship between the traffic manager and your competitor, or it could be that it is simply difficult for the potential client to make the changes and this might be in a busy shipping or receiving period. No change could be justified at this time since a change of carriers could upset the

supply of merchandise to clients or manufacturing lines. In this event a change could create an expense that would easily offset and eliminate any savings in the transportation or supply chain. There are many varieties of objections as to why a switch of supply chain providers is not desirable. Quite often the issue of rates will NOT apply, and one of the reasons you have been unsuccessful could be because you have concentrated your sales effort on the <u>wrong segment</u> in the supply chain.

The COLLABORATION Process

If you have the opportunity to sit down with your customer maybe even a Key Account, try to apply the "collaboration process".

What is really preventing us from collaborating more, does it not seem to make perfect sense to collaborate and enter into win/win situations?

Sometimes it is lack of trust between retailer, manufacturers and 3PL's. This seemed to be a main reason, but I believe that some more prominent reasons may be the difficulty or lack of integration between two or more companies. It appears to come back to the visibility issue, is it real or is it "just" a lack of assimilation of information that is simply not visible?

Could it be that the forecasting is not accurate or reliable?

Is this aspect a true consumer demand or is it driven by financial objectives?

- **Could it be that the inventory is not visible enough, planned properly or positioned correctly?**

- **Are the resources allocated by the potential collaborative partners not sufficient and some resources are held back?**

- **Are you a victim of internal "politics" and the support for the processes are not there?**

- **Could it be that the human resources are not sufficiently allocated and provided to get this collaborative process going?**

I think that this process is often driven by data or the lack of data. The willingness to collaborate could also be hindering a functional progress.

Regardless, you have to push forward to continuously work on creating a collaborative process since in the end it will need to be a win/win situation.

There are many premises for success but one is that you gain or already have a strategic understanding of your collaborative partner company. You specifically need an overall general perception of their business priorities and requirements as you start this interaction. It is imperative in order to be able to form a solid long term strategic partnership with your customer.

You should always strive to really "sit down" with your existing or new customers and try to comprehend their situation and the problems they face. This collaborative process does not include sitting down to present a rate or a new proposal, that will come later. During a session of this nature, I strongly recommend that you bring a selected team with you and urge your customer to do the same. I suggest a team since there are very few truly global sales executives that can analyze, perform and understand all ramifications of recommendations or interactions to suggest and implement a solution.

In this session you have to actually go through each step your customer is undertaking during the total supply chain. If you have done the business incubator process, you can apply those findings now.

It will be your responsibility to identify opportunities where you as a third party supplier can add value to their existing procedures. It could mean to assume some of the tasks that they are presently performing in house and take them into your infra structure.

- Who will be involved in the different processes at the various stages?

This will obviously vary within different companies however the principle has many similarities.

Please pay special attention to how the supply chain department is interacting with the various departments. Within a company there sometimes are internal points and issues that become visible. Common points that come up are lack of visibility or communication. There are a number of opportunities that you could enter into, focus and develop by recognizing these points. By being very pro-active and having this discussion and understanding such issues as lead time, you can become a virtual supply chain provider and a dependent supplier in several parts of a complex supply chain.

By establishing yourself early in the supply chain process you can rest assured of a successful and long strategic partnership.

To further elaborate on how important collaborative planning is, while I was working at a manufacturing company we were applying the rules of CPFR, Collaborate Planning Forecasting and Replenishment. This is part of getting closer to your vendors and understanding the forecasts and inventory along with actual sales and is always critical. If your customer already has an established process like this one, you can ask to take an active role and not only be the transportation/supply chain provider.

I have on several occasions met with sales executives who have said; "I don't understand, I have lowered the rate, as a matter of fact I know our rate is substantially lower and my service is better etc., why am I not getting this business?"

If you do not have the opportunity to collaboratively discuss with the potential customer you have to apply the SCM Principle and go over the supply chain in detail even if you have to assume some details.

I asked a few questions as to the product which was determined to be ready packaged consumer goods to be sold directly to a number of stores (B2B) as well as direct sales to consumer (B2C) via a website and a catalog. We analyzed the total quotation which was very comprehensive and well presented. I then suggested the "SCM Principle".

This makes you look at the total flow of goods from manufacturing facility to delivered end consumer. In this particular case it was manufactured in China, transported to Guangzhou, loaded into a container, trucked to Hong Kong and shipped to Long Beach in the USA. We established that this was the easy part and by lowering the ocean freight rate by $150.00 per 40 ft container and the customs brokerage fee with $25.00 no real saving could be derived. We then proceeded to look at the transportation to an inland location in Memphis and virtually the same was true in regards to freight savings also on this portion of the supply chain. We then evaluated the actual contents of the typical container and established the weight and size of the final shipment to the end consumer. We had suddenly discovered a "weak link" or a "critical area". This portion could potentially become more expensive and had a significant amount of manual labor attached to it. Bearing in mind that the actual costing on behalf of this importer was attached to each unit sold. The cost saving on the "bulk" transportation such as ocean freight or MLB (mini land bridge service) was not of paramount interest since the actual cost reduction was nominal per unit.

In order to obtain this business it was quickly realized that we had to come up with a solution in the actual distribution in the USA rather then trying to compete on the international transportation routes. This particular supply chain provider had very good distribution centers and a well developed courier network with a number of virtual alliances. Although the customer had not requested a complete proposal (he was too busy to pay real attention), one was developed and a request for presentation was made. The presentation was very successful and it was apparent that this customer's distribution set up had not been evaluated for some time.

This new distribution proposal would significantly reduce the cost per item. The real value add was found in a diversification of inventory with inventory close to the final consumer. As a second phase, we added a network analysis based on historic normal demand per state and placed inventory appropriately. Over and above this we introduced this customer to the volume purchased rates with UPS and FedEx and the end result was a significant saving per unit. The final piece was the systems integration and the fact that we could provide visibility throughout the supply including the last mile delivery to the end customer. We provided an upload of all parcel delivery shipments to their website with tracking so their customer service had full visibility and could correctly advise the final recipient.

The customer decided to make a switch. It made a lot of sense to give the total transaction to this one supply chain supplier particularly since a very well developed information system was attached. This system would *add overall value* and provide a more complete visibility to the customer of all his cargo moves.

You have to be able to add value to your customers' existent levels of service, or why else would he consider utilizing the services of your company.

In view of the fact that the lower ocean freight rates had already been received by the customer, the lower rates had to be honored, thereby resulting in an additional total saving to the customer. My point is, if you would have taken the "SCM Principle" into consideration from the very beginning, you may not have offered the lower rates on the ocean freight rates and spent time and effort on this since you would have obtained the total business based on the distribution proposal. You could also have kept that profit margin you now had to give away.

This particular situation clearly illustrates the fact that you do not have to lower the rate at all times to obtain the business. The specific savings or improvement of particular services could add enough value to the customer to warrant a switch to your company. Part of analyzing the supply chain also means that you have to decide where the "real" points of competition are:

- **Is this an end consumer issue with attached distribution?**

- **Is this a matter of air, truck or ocean freight or where is the <u>real</u> competitive point?**

You also have to obtain the terms of sale to find out where and who is responsible for which phase in the supply chain.

A recommendation to change the terms of purchase by using appropriate INCO terms and adjust insurance coverage to fit can be a hidden attribute. Cost savings and a demonstration of your and your company's overall understanding of the supply chain will go a long way.

I am not saying that you should give up the "typical" freight quotations, since there is a definite demand for this type of supply chain sales, however by making an attempt and asking the right questions prior to submitting a quotation, you could save yourself a lot of valuable time and increase the likelihood of obtaining more business.

In today's world with so many typical and non-typical scenarios the position and ownership of inventory can become critical.

Take a look at drop ship models which is prevalent for many ecommerce companies and try to understand where their inventory locations may be optimized and how this part of the supply chain cost can be reduced. Maybe you can offer additional services in distribution or via contract delivery features?

Another potentially emerging area is the actual ownership of the inventory and managing this often requires the services of a 3PL. This could be variations on VMI (Vendor Managed Inventory), VOI (Vendor Owned Inventory) or simply JIT (Just In Time) inventory. With VMI it is clear the vendor releases inventory against order or forecast. The VOI is sometimes a little bit trickier since the vendor now owns the inventory. An example of VOI is in the area of computers where some of these parts are used by several computer companies and they all "draw" from the same inventory. In this case the forecasting and planning aspects becomes very critical and a mistake of not having the 3PL that handles this completely organized and accurate could indeed be catastrophic.

In the JIT environment, the role as a 3PL can be extremely rewarding but here again, mistakes are very costly since the margin of error and inventory is always thin to non-existing.

When providing services for these scenarios you have to develop an extreme collaborative relationship both in systems and process or you can easily fail in providing the supply chain services and subsequently lose the business. The enabler in this aspect is system integration where there is a continuous data sharing between all of the parties. The collaborative forecasting model becomes imperative especially in the areas where owner ship or management of inventory is not in the hands of the distributor/manufacturer/retailer.

When it comes to collaborating across the supply chain, I suspect that sometimes the diverse systems between the different collaborative partners needs to be examined more closely and potential synergies to collaborate must be sought after. Failing to do so may hinder more collaboration opportunities. At times this could be the role of a 3PL to supply a better platform for the integration of technology.

Cross-channel or multichannel/ecommerce retailing is the next opportunity where many of the same processes that are generally applied in a "normal" supply chain are up for experimental and opportune processes that will enhance consumer experience.

MULTI CHANNEL RETAILER – ecommerce, how the supply chain changes

A **multichannel retailer** is a company that sells directly to the public via more than one distribution channel. The new multichannel retailers sell through "brick & mortar" retail stores, ecommerce and catalog distribution.

Typically, a multichannel retailer begins with a traditional retail storefront, then adds a mail order catalog or a web site and quickly expand the selling via the online presence as an ecommerce merchant.

Although this is a common sequence of events, there are other successful multichannel retailers who have started with either a web front or direct mail channel first. They have then expanded their marketing efforts into the "real world" of traditional retail storefront selling environments.

Establishing more than one way for their customers to shop for their products, is a method for retailers to grow their customer base, monthly revenues and gain new customers. They in turn can be marketed to via other channels not used during their initial purchase. It's not only marketing that pushed the topic to the top of retailers agenda. Nowadays more and more customers use various channels for an informed purchase decision including social media information derived from such sites as Face Book and Twitter. While they do so, they easily change channels within the purchase process. Customers just want to shop with the brand, regardless how a retailer might have organized themselves internally.

It's important that retailers support and encourage customers when they change between channels. Retailers who don't do so risk losing customers as they might wander off to a competitor who has a better presence in the other channel. Retailers must also strive to reduce disruption and confusion while customers swap channels. Both will hamper the customers purchasing process, prolonging sales cycles, with an increased risk of losing the customer all together.

However, multichannel is not a retail topic only. In fact it's a topic relevant to anyone who sells goods or services. Hence this is also relevant to importers, exporters and manufacturers that sell directly to consumers (B2C) or enterprises who sell to other businesses (B2B). In those situations customers will also use various channels for their purchase.

Disintermediation was a real concern for most retailers when they considered ecommerce, which in economics is the free market removal of intermediaries in a supply chain. This is often explained with the phrase, "cutting out the middleman". Initially, Brick and

Click companies were skeptical whether or not to add an online e-commerce channel for fear that selling their products there might produce channel conflict with their off-line retailers, agents, or their own stores. This argument has now become obsolete and internet is being added to the distribution channel portfolio after seeing how much business online competitors are generating.

From our perspective as supply chain providers we have to work with our customers to understand their requirements. If they are a retailer with "traditional" distribution points with pallet in pallet out or pallet in case out to retail stores we typically know how to manage this. However a complete change of process will be required for ecommerce B2C/B2B where individual units are picked and packed for shipping. Many of your warehouse and inventory managers will need new training to provide these services in an efficient way. Often the pure velocity of ecommerce will require a separation of process into a new area of a distribution center or a new building. The mode of transportation or combination of transportation may change due to the typically higher transaction volume of ecommerce. As a result new systems with enhanced ecommerce shipping modules are also required to provide a competitive ecommerce fulfillment service.

With this channel, often both shipping points and inventory positions will change dramatically and we must lead and design ecommerce processes to support. As free shipping becomes more prevalent the ecommerce fulfillment, transportation and inventory locations become paramount. Each aspect has to be optimized to keep fulfillment and delivery costs at a minimum.

Returns processes will also change where the purchase may have been a pure ecommerce transaction but the return is actually to a store. The reverse logistics process must be made to accommodate also this aspect and not only an ecommerce return. In general reverse logistics process typically includes the aspects of inspecting the goods, destroying/liquidating, repairing/refurbishing, re-pack and return to inventory or potentially sell via online or other auction. A 3PL can fill an important role in the reverse logistics service area.

Retail sales in stores with their higher overheads are growing year over years around the 2 – 4% while ecommerce in some cases grow at a staggering 30%. The growth in ecommerce is expected to continue.

Traditionally, and within a company, microeconomics sometimes dictates that the multi channel approach is kept independent of each other. The optimization cost cutting processes required to stay competitive in a competitive market segment used to remain within each business unit. Now, with the integrating effects of information systems across firms in complex, synergistic value chains, information is shared, and supporting supply chains are made to be transparent. Even though many of the supply chain and operational processes are integrated it is not uncommon for each business unit to operate independently with its own profit and loss statement. Global market competition reduces costs overall and supply chains have to be integrated or separated depending on each company situation and requirements.

The important issue for us in the supply chain industry is to recognize these aspects and at all times provide solutions that makes sense. The optimization that we provide within the traditional supply chains or the new ones, have now a more direct impact on the competitive aspect of using the supply chain as a competitive tool. These savings can now be more easily passed on to the end customer and we need to position our features and services accordingly.

The emergence of ecommerce companies has also developed a new type of industry which is the Drop Ship companies. This business set up is used by both pure play and established retailers. As an example many ecommerce companies do not own their inventory but rather use a drop ship system and sometimes a 3PL is used for fulfillment of these orders. The drop ship feature can also be set up with owned inventory but you allow or make arrangements with the vendor or wholesaler/distributor to drop ship on your behalf.

To illustrate, a typical B2C/B2B supply chain is composed of four or five entities (in order)

> Supplier
> Manufacturer
> Wholesaler

> ➤   Retailer
> ➤   Buyer-Customer

It has been argued that the Internet modifies the supply chain due to market transparency:

> ➤   Supplier
> ➤   Manufacturer/importer
> ➤   Buyer – Customer

The format can also be retailer, wholesaler direct to buyer-consumer. This is where a drop ship relationship exists.

As you can see in this simplified format, the supply chains are constantly changing and we must stay vigilant to understand how to separate or integrate every step observing performance and action that complies with demand.

OCEAN FREIGHT SALES

Ocean freight is historically one of the first methods of transporting any type of cargo. The use of ships became our first real commercial mode of transportation and we have used ships to transport our cargo for hundreds of years. Ocean freight shipping has since evolved into one of the most efficient and cost-effective ways to ship cargo from one point to another.

When selling ocean freight services your options have expanded appreciably. Just look at the extent of FCL (Full Container Loads) to LCL (Less then Container Loads) and the numerous variations of services and container sizes. Many vessels are designed for RO-RO (Roll on Roll of services for vehicles, dry bulk shipment or NCL (Non Conforming Loads) of heavy machinery or large pieces of equipment.

For those that considered ocean freight to be the slower method of shipping and the non time sensitive mode of transportation, think again. The new vessels are very fast and extremely large.

In terms of container capacity, several of the newer ships can load over 14,000 TEU's (20 foot container equivalent). These ships are over 350 meters (1148 feet) long and massive. Even larger ships are being built and scheduled for delivery over the next few years.

The traditional 3PL's or International Freight Forwarders are

 selling their ocean freight services by signing contracts for container shipping with the ocean carriers. They in turn are reselling these containers to their customers as FCL and LCL services.

The industry is changing very rapidly and what was once a matter of selling the ocean freight rate to your customer has now become part of an expansive supply chain service. The matter of only selling

"port-to-port" services is becoming less frequent and the "door-to-door" solution is now more prominent.

3PL's and Freight Forwarders will operate as OTI (Ocean Transport Intermediary) or call themselves a NVOCC (Non Vessel Operating Common Carrier).

We have traditionally seen them take a leading role in the sale of this transportation arm. Over recent years the ocean carriers themselves are selling directly to their clients as well. The carriers are embracing the total supply chain concept and have either invested in infrastructure in selected markets or formed strategic alliances with other 3PL's. By using strategic alliances they can quickly grow, establish themselves in this market and provide services door to door.

The technology aspect of supply chain visibility is addressed in an aggressive way and like 3PL's they are providing supply chain visibility via software applications. These software tools are designed to interact with ERP, WMS, TMS and other management software.

This is becoming a big picture process and I believe that the personal intervention by a trained 3PL sales executive is required to provide the personal touch and knowledge.

The personal approach is often consultative advice such as choice of container and understanding loading patterns to optimize the capacity of the container.

I recently utilized a Container Load Building Software for some of my customers. The graphic design of the load patterns proved to be very useful and assisted when the container was loaded. I found that this additional service carried a lot of goodwill and saved the customer significantly.

By adding special crating for the portion that did not fit into the full containers additional benefits were derived when shipping LCL. These simple value-add tools create that personal touch and demonstrates knowledge.

The import services needs to extend not only to your customer's suppliers but also beyond to ensure a truly uninterrupted supply chain. The services must include all the inland services to securely transport the cargo to the final destination. The idea is to provide a seamless service that is all inclusive end to end.

There are many different requirements for supply chains but time versus cost still prevails as one of the most important aspects. To demonstrate reliability some ocean freight forwarders are even offering a money back guarantee if the cargo does not arrive on time.

The rate calculator sites that exist for ocean freight are very common and ocean rates are readily available. As an ocean sales executive you must be up to date on all of your rates. Sometimes the way to sell against lower rates on the internet is to "combine" other services thus increasing the overall customer value proposition.

Current economic conditions have "forced" companies to keep inventory levels low. Others have strategically elected to keep the inventory levels low. One reason for this is to avoid tying up capital and increase capital reserves. When inventories are kept this low and a sudden increase in supply is required, ocean freight is often too slow and air freight is too expensive.

In these instances suggest a sea-air alternative. Sea-Air has been an option for many years but not everyone is selling this service. This combines ocean freight and airfreight where the cargo is flown part of the way and shipped by ocean the other part. The cost is as the name suggests somewhere between air and ocean and can serve as a viable alternative.

It is up to a qualified and properly trained 3PL sales executive that understands ocean freight to design services that are suitable for every situation and customer. Gone are the days when it was an issue of just selling a rate attached to a basic service. You need to understand the total supply chain to be successful.

TRUCK SALES

The trucking industry is a very important part of any supply chain. The different modes of trucking from dry van, flat bed, FTL, LTL to parcel allows for optimization within any transportation segment.

By taking a closer look at where trucking services typically occur within the supply chain, you can quickly recognize the importance of trucks. Here are a few segments where trucks in one form or another (FTL, LTL, Flatbed, Refrigerated, Bulk etc.) are supporting the movement of product and material between;

- **Port to DC or terminal – import or export**

- **Intermodal – to and from rail ramp**

- **DC and Store**

- **Manufacturing plant and DC**

- **Parcel distribution**

- **DC to consumer**

- **Store to consumer**

- **DC to jobsite**

- **DC to DC**

- **Cross border delivery**

When it comes to choosing a dry van trucking provider, there are a large variety for both regional and national carriers. Depending on what your customer wants you need to select the most optimal solution.

This could mean a single truck load for this one time or an integrated program that would support a total supply chain.

The employ of truck brokers and website rate and carrier choice are prevalent in this industry and with good reason. The truck rates have over the years evolved and many variations of rates depending on region and national coverage exist. To maneuver these tariffs and class rates can be difficult. These web routing and rating engines are commonly available to assist you to pick the best rate. Over and above we have a number of transportation brokers in this very competitive environment.

Even though flexibility, consistency, availability and on time delivery may be obvious on web sites, the personal touch and expertise is always needed.

Selling truck services with rates, routes, equipment availability and dependable service is one aspect, but the value add to actual physical process when loading and offloading is another. A simple task of being able to confirm these processes to a customer is of highest importance. If you are trucking freight from a DC or terminal, just to go over your truck inspection process will demonstrate that you have an established reliable process and you are not just "trucking" the freight.

If you are selling LTL service, with multi-stops, the value-add feature may be that you have a well developed route optimization software that will ensure on time performance.

Other process that you may mention could relate to your staging process prior to shipping. Load planning, route optimization, product loading and packaging processes are sometimes another differentiator in obtaining the business.

Since I have been very involved in the refrigerated trucking business, the value added tasks of always inspecting the reefer as it comes to load is important. To double check that the cooler unit is working properly is one aspect. To measure temperature inside the van as you open the doors is another safety measure.

Providing temperature readers with the load is just as important and making certain the cooling unit maintained the temperature during the total transit time is a must.

By incorporating these simple processes into SOP's (Standard Operating Process) you have increased your customers trust in you and potentially made your relationship stronger.

Trucking industry is an important part of the visibility within the supply chain. The technology is readily available and many trucks are now equipped with GPS, Satellite tracking and Qualcomm communications. Many trucking companies provide this service for the customer to monitor their trucks via a website. This service can include confirmation of delivery at each destination.

As a 3PL or trucking company, this technology allows you to benchmark your operations; select appropriate KPI's and measure your success rate on a regular basis.

To be on time with the correct truck and service, you should be informed of the total supply chain and have visibility to the different transportation segments. As companies are optimizing their inventory locations, you as a trucker should support their efforts.

The importance of collaborating on timing and services with your customers has never been more important. As your customers are obtaining more visibility into their own supply chains, your service support becomes an integrated part that must be synchronized with the rest of the supply chain.

- I have said this before, any disruption in the supply chain at any segment, will have "ripple" effects in every aspect and you do not want to be the cause for disruption.

Although there are many regional and local trucking organizations that are very effective in what they do many trucking companies are taking a deeper look into the supply chain. They are providing comprehensive supply chain services through their own operations and increasingly forming alliances by well thought out partnerships.

These new partnerships effectively enables this part of the supply chain to become an active part to lead and enhance overall supply chain activities.

WARHOUSING AND DISTRIBUTION SALES

Warehousing and distribution is becoming more vital as the demands for quicker delivery is increasing. The warehouse locations must be close to your customers or you can lose your competitiveness. The cost to deliver quicker can become insurmountable and inefficient.

In order to sustain a competitive advantage many warehouse and distribution centers have invested in significant infrastructure. This will include their dynamic layout of racks and floor space along with technology.

Numerous 3PL's have a variety of warehouses that are designed to handle different types of material. This could mean that the warehouse is set up to receive an ocean container, rail car, truck, air cargo shipment or inbound parcels where they inventory and re-ship in single units or full pallets.

Their systems must be designed to manage each and every one of these different types of cargo or to become a dedicated facility for a specific requirement or commodity.

As a sales executive in this area you must have a thorough understanding of material handling processes applicable for a specific cargo and how a DC (distribution center) physically handles the product.

There are a number of different types of warehousing/DC's. These DC's can be dedicated/contract warehouse or shared/public warehouses.

Some are classified under the following subsections;

- Food graded, grocery

- Refrigerated

- Bulk

- ecommerce and rapid fulfillment

- General merchandise

- Hazardous

Some typical "standard" services that DC's provide are;

- Inventory management

- Retail and Manufacturing distribution

- Pick and Pack

- Kitting

- Cross Docking

- Assembly processes – sub or light

- Packaging

- Consolidation and de-consolidation

- Import/Export services

- Reverse Logistics

- Inspection and lot control

- Transportation services

- Parcel shipping services

There may even be a need to utilize a warehouse that has a Free Trade Zone (FTZ) feature. A FTZ is a secured area that is located on US soil (many countries around the world have this category of FTZ). The FTZ is still considered to be outside the US commerce and as such not required to pay duty and excise taxes until the goods is released into commerce for consumption. There is no time limit on how long the goods can be in a FTZ and if the goods is re-exported no duty is payable since it never entered the US commerce.

Work and assembly can also be done on the goods while in FTZ which may or may not alter its foreign content for duty applications.

If the rate on foreign inputs admitted/assembled in the zone is higher then the rate applied to the finished product the FTZ user may choose the finished product rate, thereby reducing amount of duty owed. Many cars are manufactured in a FTZ environment.

To properly sell the services of a selected DC you should have a good understanding of what the total supply chain is and what the exact customer requirements are.

Most DC's are located within reasonable distance to major population centers and the perimeters for delivery or pick up of product must be defined.

- Is the warehouse equipped with a rail ramp, is it close to intermodal rail facilities and major highways?

- Is it required that delivery is performed next day or does a two day delivery suffice?

- Do you have competitive rates and sufficient transportation available?

- Does the DC require that new supply chain lanes or vendors need to be considered?

- Is this a slow moving SKU (Stock Keeping Unit) in pallet quantity?

- Is the choice of this location the only DC required or are there other existing DC's being utilized?

- How is forecasting and fulfillment going to change with this new DC?

- Inventory levels and turns?

- Compilation of SKU's?

- Will there be a requirement to cross dock or deconsolidate?

- Is this a pallet in and case or item out?

- Can the DC handle any peak season activities or special events both from an operational point of view and labor?

Depending on the real circumstances there may be many more items that you may need to be considering.

You have to be well informed when it comes to the technology and the systems that this DC has.

Does it have full suite WMS, is it a tier one or tier two system, is it a legacy system, is it sufficient to handle the volume and customer requirements?

Customer requirements are a major part of systems together with visibility. Reporting is a prerequisite and it is imperative to meet or exceed customer expectations.

Is a TMS (Transportation Management System) and YMS (yard Management System) in place?

What will it take to integrate this system to the customers systems and other supply chain software products?

These are just some high level points to be considered and it is a prerequisite that you are totally aware of these considerations.

Any mistake or where a system or process does not work will have a ripple effect into the supply chain inbound or outbound.

When you as supply chain sales executive sell these services, there must be a comprehensive understanding of the total process.

The senior management of your customer and your company must be committed and completely aware of risks, costs and benefits.

- **Change is never easy, but in an ever evolving supply chain, it is inevitable.**

AIR FREIGHT SALES

The first airplanes to have scheduled cargo shipments were for airmail post in 1911. The routes were not many but pioneered in England, Germany and in California during the same year. The services gradually expanded over the next years. This was a humble but exciting start of air cargo as we know it today.

In the beginning a few bags of mail was the extent of the maximum payload.

Today's aircrafts have very impressive payloads and cargo volumes.

An Airbus A400M can carry around 82,000 lbs (37,000 kg) while a Boeing 747-8F can hand 30,000 cu ft (1840 m3) with a payload of 295,800 lbs (134,200 kg). To look at larger aircrafts you have to note the Antonov 225 with a payload of 550,000 lbs (250,000 kg) which is an almost unbelievable amount to be flown.

Air cargo is sometimes related to emergency shipments and to be avoided if at all possible. This may not always be the case since certain cargo is more suitable for air cargo then ocean freight or truck. Typically high priced and/or perishable items that are small in size and costly to keep in inventory are ideal candidates for air cargo shipments. Specific airfreight programs are often designed especially for JIT supply chains.

As a 3PL and freight forwarder the consolidated airfreight service is most often promoted. This reduces the straight airline rate for single shipments and is an obvious choice to lower transportation costs.

The courier companies have a variety of different levels of services to allow for lower cost structures such as next day air, two and three day air.

Since jet fuel is expensive, space on aircraft is limited and operating expenses are high, many of these air services are not being flown anymore.

When the couriers started out in air business, they had a strategic rule of the hub and spoke system. Everything flew in and out of the spoke and the service was flawless and an all air product. The service for these courier companies is still flawless but the hub and spoke system was abandoned many years ago.

Many next, two and three day air shipments are now trucked wherever it makes sense. Their ground network is very sophisticated and the on time performance is in the high 90% most of the time. This makes good sense from both operating expenses and environmental aspects. Sustainability and green process are making significant headway in these areas.

When you as a sales executive sell airfreight a part of your sales pitch should be about reliability, frequency and a lower cost then expected. If you couple the speed of airfreight with consistent door to door service you have a good sales argument.

The cost for airfreight has to be carefully defined including terminal, handling, pick up, delivery and customs clearance fees. Since this is as competitive as other services you need to make sure that your rates are up to date.

When you quote airfreight rates, the issues of dimensions are critical as dimensional charges are costly and it can also make a difference when you try to fit cargo into an air container. Packaging should be evaluated as part of your service.

When you sell your air freight services, I find it to be good practice to include the type and choice of air carriers you are using and potentially indicate their on time performance.

Many countries also have significant documentary requirements which you must be certain to explain and promote as a service you provide.

Your service performance should be benchmarked and measured on a continuous basis to ensure that the customer understands that the service is in line with the commitment.

When I was responsible for Gateway Computers supply chain I had the unfortunate experience of shortage of inventory. This was a

JIT (Just In Time) supply chain and any miscalculations by any vendor required a decisive and sometimes creative solution.

This happened when a vendor or supplier was late or a transportation provider failed to meet the schedule. I had issues of lost containers, lost trucks, bad weather, air craft change that forced our cargo to be left behind and many other unusual situations.

The driving factor in my case was that if the parts did not make it to the production line on time a $50,000 per hour cost would be factual. I resorted to re-routing freight or changing mode of transportation from ocean freight to airfreight. I routinely spent extra money on dedicated team trucks, just to make sure the trucks would not stop for any reason whatsoever. Every aspect of a potential delay anywhere in the supply chain had to be evaluated and removed if it poised any risk of delay.

Contingency planning was done at every instant and prepared ahead of time, just in case something went wrong. Regardless how much you plan and prepare contingency plans of action, you cannot anticipate every issue.

My big resolution when it was absolutely critical was to charter an aircraft. I compared the cost of chartered aircraft to down time of production and loss of revenue. I made several decisions to charter air crafts based on this cost benefit analysis.

The mode of air cargo was for me in these instances the resolution and although costly overall it saved thousands of dollars. The fact that we never closed down the production for supply chain reasons contributed greatly to a continued positive customer experience. Satisfied customers come back and revenues will continue to grow.

The really time sensitive shipments can of course also be submitted to one of the worldwide courier companies.

DHL has traditionally been in front of the international air freight/parcel shipments but both FedEx and UPS have made substantial inroads. If you look at all of these carriers investment in air crafts and other infrastructure you know that they are very serious about international airfreight. The service guarantees with money back speaks to this fact as well.

Sometimes the commodity and nature of goods has to be reviewed and in the case of hazardous cargo special forms has to be filled out and packaging requirements must be met without fail and certain cargo can only fly on all cargo air crafts.

On April the 1st some years ago, I was working in Switzerland and I had just arrived there. My German had some serious "flaws", but overall I managed to communicate well. I received a phone call from a new customer that wanted to book 2000 kilos of "radio wellen". Even though I was not quite sure what this really was I accepted the booking and proceed to make the arrangements. My colleagues provided me with a vague translation. I contacted the airlines to book the space but was laughed at. The reason was that the real translation of "radio wellen" was radio waves and if you ever try to pack or ship this it would prove to be rather difficult....

Did you notice it was April the 1st..... and my colleagues just had some fun with my German language abilities.

As I found out this was tradition to do to the new foreign person and I had my chance for retribution the following year. I arranged for this new person whose German wasn't that good either to book "button holes"....

The reason I mention this is that it is very important to truly understand all requirements and not accept something you do not comprehend. Because of speed and significant security requirements airfreight is less forgiving and can cause serious issues.

The airfreight portion is an expensive part of any supply chain and must be treated as such and margins and room for error is much smaller then an ocean or truck shipment.

PARCEL AND COURIER SALES

In this book I have to some degree focused on ecommerce and the importance of the supporting supply chains. Most ecommerce supply chains contain parcel shipping for B2C or B2B. The opportunity to successfully integrate parcel sales into the rest of the supply chain is phenomenal.

When you are thinking about parcel shipping you automatically think a UPS, FedEx, USPS and DHL. They play a dominant role in the market. If you sell for them your customers are already very familiar with your company. If you on the other hand represent some of the lesser know parcel carriers such as regional carriers your sales presentation will need to be more "educational" and elaborate on your service offering.

I still believe that you need to understand the total supply chain in order to be truly effective even in the parcel sales portion. We know UPS and FedEx both have added Supply Chain capabilities and can manage virtually the total supply chain end to end. DHL has traditionally concentrated on international and since they acquired Danzas many years ago DHL has true end to end capabilities as well.

If we concentrate on the parcel sales aspect, both the customer and the sales executive should focus on what makes this the best relationship from an operational process and a costs perspective.

As a parcel representative, you have to be acutely aware that most shippers with some significance in their shipping volumes will negotiate to use a second or a third carrier as well. The old process of playing one against the other is still a good option.

I believe the discussion should be around optimization at all times and not about yield for the carriers shipping lane. I recognize that you have a responsibility in this aspect as well but a higher degree of collaboration with your customer could still provide this benefit. Once you work with your customer to review every angle of the relationship you can truly get an optimization that is sustainable.

As an example, work with the customers packaging make sure the dimensions are clearly defined and understood so you can avoid that *"dreadful"* dimensional weight application. If you are faced with the "dimensional factor" try to get a dim factor change. Sometimes this will work however it is becoming rarer. Once you start this discussion, and if the dim factor reduction is not an option, the parcel pricing unit may provide other discounts in order to reduce the overall freight expense.

The actual packaging itself is often somewhat neglected in negotiations. Particularly when you are talking to a shipper with more fragile or regulated commodities such as certain Pharma or even hazardous material. I think a better rate can be negotiated if the packaging is correct from a material handling aspect so your damage ratio can be justifiably lower then average.

If the dimensions are good, fits into your yield you should also be able to provide a more competitive rate.

I am a big advocate of non cardboard and non-petroleum based materials and have for a long time promoted BIO degradable packaging. When you discuss packaging with a customer make sure to explain that the package is subject to several types of sorters where handling is strictly mechanical and damages will occur if the packaging is inadequate. The fact that many shippers print fragile and this side up is in real life no guarantee for special handling or

that a parcel will travel the "right" side up on a conveyor belt. Some of our bigger parcel shippers will be sorting millions of packages per day so how can you make sure that any specific package receives special handling.

Even when the delivery trucks are loaded it means virtually nothing as to how the package is marked. Typically heavier packages will be put in lower racks in the truck, but that is no guarantee that a smaller package will not be put there as well. In this case the smaller package must support the weight of many other packages so your packaging "specifications" must be in line with this situation. Regardless, there will never be a guarantee that the parcel will not be stacked "upside down" inside a delivery truck.

I just think that an open conversation by you as a parcel sales executive about packaging is necessary and that it will create a lot of goodwill. Drop test and other features should be part of this discussion, just to make sure you service your customer the best possible way.

The "last mile" delivery is almost always the most critical part of a parcel delivery process. As an example, if you have a perishable product that is either heat or cold sensitive, your exposure is potentially the highest during the "last mile". Since most parcel delivery trucks are not insulated the heat or the cold will be significant during this time and the product damage is real.

I have designed many Zone Jump processes for perishable B2C shipments be it for fruit, chocolate or flowers. In these cases the carriers did accept our trucks since we refrigerated the bulk shipment to the hub where it would be injected thus protecting the product as long as possible. The "last mile" is however where the protection is most required so it made sense to Zone Jump refrigerated. This way we would allow the packaging, the gel paks or dry ice to really perform during the "last mile" where the exposure and risk for damage is the greatest.

I have on many occasions asked for common sense on behalf of the delivery driver to place the parcel where it is not so severely exposed to either heat or cold. I will gladly give those "last mile" delivery professionals kudos because common sense still prevails.

Overwhelmingly they do their best and try to protect the product as much as possible. They typically try placing the parcel out of direct sunlight or protect it from freezing winds. In either of these cases packaging becomes really important.

The shippers are getting smarter and smarter and many new and old techniques in parcel shipping must be sold. As briefly mentioned above, take Zone Skipping or Zone Jump as an example. This has been practiced by many for several years but I think some sales proposals are omitting this aspect unless the customer specifically asks for this service. This can be a tremendous saving compared to next day or any air product.

For those of you that are not familiar with zone jump, this means trucking a large number of parcels fitted for next day ground delivery from a certain hub. The truck "injects" the parcels at the destination hub. It is a zip code sorting issue and you must have order management software designed to handle sorting zip codes to a next day ground delivery network. This may also require a more sophisticated shipping system that can process both sorting and correct origin label. As a matter of fact a properly designed shipping system will create significant savings and provide an accurate shipping process. Carriers also prefer these systems since the level of accuracy is very high.

I know internally within the carriers, they don't necessarily want all kinds of shippers to send their own truckers to their hubs since this would quickly become a nightmare to handle. However most parcel shipping companies now have their own trucking service and can provide their own trucks to fit into their required delivery process.

The Zone Jump process needs to be explored even more as Free Shipping becomes more prominent.

Free Shipping will to a greater degree create an optimized process for where your inventory should be placed in relation to your end recipient. More and more customers are looking for that next day gratification of free shipping and unless you can deliver <u>next day</u> **<u>ground</u>** for a majority of your parcels your delivery expense will increase dramatically. This is predominantly true for B2C shipments but this is becoming as important with B2B.

When you are talking to a parcel customer, make sure to understand how they fulfill their orders and identify if there are any potential bottlenecks in their process?

Are there any issue or process that would prevent them from having the total shipping volume ready when you need to pick it up?

In case of large volumes, work collaboratively with your customer to see if a "pre-sort" can be done to better accommodate your local sort of parcels. The frequency as to when you can physically pick up orders can often become an important issue so it is important to have a properly designed schedule for any larger volume shipper.

Are there any other supply issues or expected shortages that can affect shipping volumes?

One of the most important aspects of shipping parcels is the systems or lack of systems. Will it suffice to implement your own, carrier system, or is it not possible whereas the customer already has their own shipping system. If they have their own system, what are the integration requirements and what are the time lines to implement?

A good shipping system will provide the carrier with accurate information, proper rating, labels, barcodes etc., so this is really a win/win situation. It will typically provide for ease of rate or zip code changes and generally avoid costly re-rating and additional invoicing with customer confrontational disputes. The shipping system vendors will keep their systems up to date with all required changes and ongoing updates and upgrades.

Some of these systems will also provide you with an auditing model to equip you with the tools to audit your parcel carriers. This audit can be from an invoicing aspect but also on time delivery performance and other data.

The technology aspect is imperative to understand since this can really make or break a new relationship. What I mean here is not only the shipping system aspect but also other systems that may indirect or directly affect the process. This could be their WMS, ERP, MRP or other internal legacy or maybe their financial software. For this reason alone it is important that you as a parcel sales executive be reasonably up dated on what the different systems do and how they interact. It is imperative to understand the actual technology, the process the shipping options and also the invoicing process that should become part of a technology solution.

Many larger companies have a very busy IT department and the supply chain area is not commonly receiving proper allocation of resources. This is why it is imperative to have full commitment from your customer even on a higher management level.

When it comes to the systems applications the data that is required for measuring the effectiveness and the costs of parcel shipping you must be sure to offer proper reports. This falls within the normal KPI's that you already have, but are there other aspects of data accumulation that may be required?

Besides of data that drives cost benefit analysis you will have to see what can best provide visibility, tracking and tracing for the customer. Does the data upload to their CRM or customer service module?

- Being proactive and benchmarking this total process makes good sense especially if your intention is to establish a long term relationship with your customer.

Even as manufacturers and retailers seek to control costs and drive efficiency across supply chains and parcel shipping the financial impact of returns and unsalable goods is significant. This opens up the avenue of selling returns and reverse logistics services which is an additional process that will dictate a new set of systems and label applications. The costs for returns and the inspection for returned products is a significant opportunity for you as a 3PL.

Keeping in mind that many inbound supply chains require parcel service and next day air or second day air is required. As the ground networks are becoming more developed and reliable, there are significant opportunities to bring some of those air packages to ground service. Yes I recognize that this may dilute some of your air.

It is however not a good sales practice to avoid these issues be it for inbound or outbound shipping lanes. You must be the first one to suggest optimization and collaborate to improve a customer's process and shipping lanes.

Any consultant or internal audit process will soon enough discover these aspects and if you have tried to get "away" with this you will most probably lose the business.

I personally acted as consultant for a significant parcel shipper and went through this exercise. I found that the parcel carrier had elected to allow both two and three day air services to ship without converting to ground and as such not optimized. The local representative was to a high degree responsible for this since his commissions were based on actual revenue. Needless to say, I fired this parcel company employed a new service provider, inserted a zone jump program, and converted as much air as I could to ground service. The cost savings were tremendous but it did not affect the delivery performance in any way.

I should not omit to mention the pricing and the final proposals. I think that many sales executives just highlights the rates per zone but does not go into the fine print. Not enough time is spent on the details including the assessorial fees which can become substantial. This is a clear opportunity for the many consultants that specialize in this area to really get hold of the carriers "tricks". By being proactive and spending more time with the customer you can create a better understanding of the proposal. You need to spend time on the fine print and explain in detail. If you are successful in this respect potentially a consultant will not be invited, simply because the customer already has a good understanding and comfort level with the proposal.

This in itself is becoming a contentious issue and one such consultant filed suit against both UPS and FedEx for alleged colluded efforts by both these carriers. The statement is allegedly suggesting that both carriers are trying to remove these third party consultants for avoidance of carrier revenue dilution. The matter is going to court in early 2012 so we all have to wait and see what the details will bring us.

ECOMMERCE SUPPLY CHAINS

Opportunity for 3PL's and other service providers

The ecommerce supply chains are representing a new opportunity for a 3PL service provider. This is emerging and the velocity of these supply chains are more rapid and most often labeled as "pull" supply chains where the end recipient influences the supply chain. This holds especially true in a B2C ecommerce process where the consumer is the demand factor.

- I wanted to share what an ecommerce company must go through to become operational to better illustrate and provide a more in depth understanding. I am hopeful that you can gain a quick insight to the process and apply your own company's process and services, or to simply see opportunity in either of these processes.

Ecommerce revenues continues to accelerate for retailers and spending by consumers through internet purchases are increasing.

70% of consumers prefer to shop online at retailers that have both online and physical stores.

Last Christmas Kohl's reported their 2010 Web sales compared to the previous December were up 66% and Macy's reported their web sales increased 28.8%.

Ecommerce revenues are increasing for most retailers although not as aggressively with double digit growth in all merchandise categories.

Kohl's claims the ability to operationally handle high e-Commerce volumes was a result of investments in technology and distribution facilities.

Macy's has similar points and is adding a 1,3 million sq ft facility in West Virginia to handle the e-Commerce growth.

The majority of consumers who use the Internet, 63.5%, went online to shop for the holidays. Over 5 % of those shoppers bought exclusively online throughout the season.

Ecommerce is continuing to grow again and sales increased some 15% year over year in June 2011 This was the eighth straight month of double-digit growth, and the 23rd month in a row that online purchases have grown.

Leading retailers are continuing to implement solutions to increase value and revenue through e-Commerce and multichannel sales. Those companies that have not yet ventured into this most lucrative channel continue to struggle with the difficulty of moving forward into an area which is very different from the traditional brick & mortar business model.

Often, hesitation to move forward to become an etailer is due to unresolved questions such as:

> What level of increased sales and profitability should be expected through introduction of an ecommerce capability?

> Can I make the business case for adding a direct to consumer channel to my existing Retail Store model?

> Without an in-house executive resource with ecommerce experience, how do I get put a Team together to start developing the needed processes and systems?

Some other aspects that retailers not yet in the ecommerce sales channel are concerned with are how to;

1. **Create business process, implementation plan, identify capital expense, resources, IT, merchandising, marketing and time required to go live.**

2. **Identify ecommerce IT Platform**

3. **Create Online Store with appropriate content**

4. **Design and implement Operational processes to support ecommerce retail**

- ➢ Fulfillment process

- ➢ System requirements

- ➢ Evaluate and recommend how to integrate ecommerce fulfillment

- ➢ Merge with existing Distribution Center or create new

- ➢ Outsource to 3PL

- ➢ Returns of merchandise to store or Distribution Center

- ➢ Call centers; set up ecommerce training – out source or in house

- ➢ Supply chain solutions for inventory – outsource or in house

- ➢ Design delivery process to consumer – outside expertise required

- ➢ Set up of UPS/FedEx/USPS/regional carriers

As you can see there are a number of areas where supply chain expertise in one form or another is required.

These are some areas where you as a 3PL can render a value proposition and insert your services. If you are successful to render services at an early stage your chances of growing with this company is significantly increased.

Naturally there are many startup companies that just never make it but in cases where a retailer is already established with store fronts, the likelihood of success is greater.

Even the "regular" pure etailers, distribution and wholesalers that enter into ecommerce will need to consider a myriad of different solutions. Some which will need an outsourced 3PL or other supply chain services.

I assisted an emerging ecommerce company that was well funded and needed my expertise to go live and start selling as soon as possible.

I have outlined some of the processes and I suggest you follow the different activities and establish where you as a 3PL, ocean carrier, trucker, courier, software or consultant can apply your services.

After the review of their business plan, budgets and what they had already accomplished in terms of website, product offering, systems and staffing I created action plans to become fully operational.

Many of these tasks were performed concurrently and I will set aside this fact to better describe what is required.

The website of their choice had an open source platform and offered a large degree of flexibility. Code and coding of software is often synonymous with flexibility and customization. I caution that it is typically not a good idea to customize and write excessive amounts of your own code. Software upgrades are always coming and too much customization will hinder upgrades.

They would have two aspects of fulfillment one would be via their own inventory and one via drop ship arrangements. Their product offering was very large and it would be too costly to purchase and keep all inventory by themselves thus the decision to drop ship a certain portion of selected items.

A drop ship program means that you will forecast your sales to an established retailer, wholesaler or distributor that will ship your order as you take the actual order on your website. The drop ship vendor can be set up so it looks like the shipment is coming directly from you.

The ecommerce platform they had selected allowed for several choices of drop ship software and a critical selection process was developed arriving at the most suitable solution.

I went over all requirements in respect to email notifications of order being shipped be it from their inventory or from a drop shipper to ensure a positive customer experience at all times.

An OMS, Order management system was put in place together with a WMS, Warehouse Management system and designed so orders could be properly allocated. On top of that I designed an order allocation process to consider delivery carriers, rate shopping/optimization, inventory location and levels of inventory.

Since their volume was to be rather large it was decided that a transactional shipping system needed to be added, so we created a process to select the most suitable software vendor for this purpose.

This system was then integrated with their WMS, Warehouse Management system. Here we selected a system that was in the cloud and no "real" software had to be purchased. Instead we purchased user licenses for the management team to use. The actual system resided with the software vendor.

So at this time we had the systems being implemented and tested. The test phase is very important which has to include a simulated stress test for peak shipping for Christmas.

During this time we set up and confirmed the Far East vendors and that they were ready to ship on time. We had to make sure our inventory did not arrive too early. An early arrival of inventory would mean an extra expense that could be avoided if the planning was done correctly.

We went over a number of 3PL vendors to select the service providers for the ocean freight and also see if the same 3PL could handle the air freight as well. The air freight rates and services were not competitive so we ended up adding a separate air freight company. All inbound supply chains were carefully evaluated for optimized time and shipping costs.

The 3PL's we used for ocean freight were also selected as customs brokers. They undertook a complete evaluation and classification for the products to ensure we understood all duties and taxes.

Since their infrastructure at this stage did not include actual warehousing and distribution facilities I had to select a 3PL based on the total supply chain requirement.

In these cases I typically consider these supply chains a "pull" environment where the end customer in one way or another actually dictates how this is going to be designed.

Since this was a new company with no history, we did delivery modeling based on typical demographic location of the general population. We also considered the actual size and dimensions of the average order and proceeded to decide where we should place inventory.

It is no secret that FREE shipping is going to prevail over the next future of ecommerce. The consumer is virtually demanding free shipping or shipping to be part of the purchase price. To make an error in inventory positioning or not optimizing for lowest possible delivery cost could indeed be a very expensive error.

In order for the merchandisers in this company to understand this aspect we calculated the cost delivery with UPS, FedEx, USPS and/or regional carriers to provide a cost that could be included in their margins. This cost would have to be considered up front and based on a potential FREE shipping promotion. Once this cost structure was understood we proceeded to engage a 3PL within the selected geographic areas to decide where the final inventory locations should be. In this case one inventory location would not suffice, especially bearing in mind that this company would be participating in the FREE shipping promotions and the last mile delivery cost would be too expensive.

I have to make a statement that not all warehouse operations and facilities are designed, nor do the personnel have the skill set, experience or operational systems to handle the higher velocity of ecommerce. This in turn limited our choice and made the selection process more difficult.

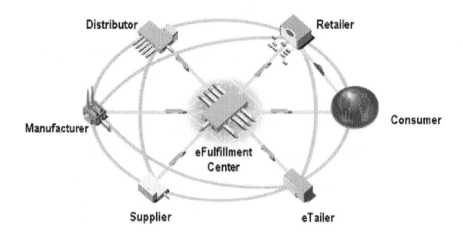

Footnote: This is one example of a multichannel set up.

I had to segregate the 3PL's that had a client mix of typical retail clients with the pallet in, pallet out and case pick only. The assumption would be that some of them were simply not designed for ecommerce fulfillment.

Since there are a number of pure play ecommerce solution fulfillment companies, those were given extra review and consideration.

As a 3PL sales executive you would have to clearly understand that because of the pure number of shipments, there must be processes that can accommodate rush shipments, late order receipt and early pick up times by the parcel shipping companies.

Many 3PL's claim to have a shipping system that can handle ecommerce shipping but when you take a closer look, their WMS system is rather basic and many features as available in a full scale shipping system are simply not present.

This was carefully reviewed to make sure that their system could actually handle the highest peak shipping day.

I reviewed the actual pick process to see if they would pick to light via their WMS set up, or have a pick to cart or some sort of wave picking to handle the volumes. I in addition looked at the frequency of picking and how their system would handle depletion of inventory in case it was not real time.

The next step in this was to go over packaging. I reviewed the packaging for the master cartons that came from the Far East and found some room for improvement. After having made some calculations and reverse engineered the packaging; I quickly discovered that it was possible to reduce the size of the master carton. This resulted in an optimized pattern for the container loading and I recommended the use of a high cube container instead.

I proceeded to evaluate the ecommerce packing and made certain that when an order had multiple line items the correct process was in place to pick the smallest possible box. For some of the really perishable smaller items I introduced our own specialty packaging designed for this purpose.

The 3PL was additionally required to present their labor picture to provide us with some comfort of available labor at peak shipping times.

In reality I made the proper statements in regards to actual shipping volumes bearing in mind this company had no history and forecast was based on the very best estimations and marketing consumer data.

The next step was to negotiate with the parcel companies to make sure I had a clear understanding of delivery times and costs. I also evaluated our potential rates against the rates currently available through the 3PL.

Reverse logistics is sometimes a section that does not receive the attention it deserves. This could represent an additional revenue source for which a very specific process has to be designed. The returns process in itself requires inspection of returned goods and all business processes and facts must be documented properly. The importance is to facilitate a good customer experience even when they return the product for any reason. This must be carefully designed. You don't want to lose a potential return customer over the reverse logistics process.

I proceeded to put out an RFP Request For Proposal for call center and customer service requirements. Most call centers today have 24-7 coverage and it will come down to their systems, the time to train, call cost per minute and response time. Here again, their ability to support call volume during peak must be assessed.

Even though an ecommerce supply chain has many similar requirements, it is often more sensitive to both transit time and costs. The inventory has to typically turn quicker and the costs throughout the supply chain for transportation, fulfillment and delivery must be interrelated, defined and clearly visible. Cost savings must be either allocated as additional profit margin or be passed on to the customer as rebates and promotional savings.

The decision on how to segregate or combine the different supply chains has to be made on an individual basis keeping in mind internal processes, demand, time in transit, cost and allocation of products at time of sale.

Under certain circumstances it may make sense to start out combining the supply chains when the ecommerce sales volumes are small and later separate them as the ecommerce portion of the business increases. Regardless, supply chain strategies have to align customer value propositions by product group and sales channel to achieve a differentiated performance level in line with sales velocity.

Recently Wal-Mart decided to align and combine the ecommerce and retail store channel and merge them by creating one senior manager responsible for both channels. The assumption behind this is to create an atmosphere of selling without internal competition between the channels. The motto is as long as it is sold by Wal-Mart it is better then through the competitors. It is not known if this actually means the supply chains merge or if they are kept separate.

When savings from efficiencies in any supply can be passed on the customer, you can truly say that you are competing by using the supply chain effectively.

The opportunities imbedded in the ecommerce business weather this is a start up or an established retailer can become significant. You can by positioning your services correctly sell more services and increase your revenues if you truly have an in depth understanding of the total process.

These are some of the high level issues that have to be considered when entering into ecommerce. There are many more side items that do not impact the supply chain directly but are still very relevant to the operational success of an ecommerce company.

SUPPLY CHAIN SYSTEMS

Although we all talk about supply chain visibility many of us still have limited visibility.

The difficulties in forecasting, planning as well as unsatisfactory inventory and order visibility makes managing a supply chain more difficult. When you extend these concerns over manufacturers, wholesalers, distributor, suppliers, vendors, transportation providers and anyone else in the supply chain, it creates a complex environment.

For successful execution of a supply chain the need for visibility and in some cases disclosure of forecasts and other business drivers are paramount for successful collaboration. Without collaboration and including key decision makers the chances of creating a truly optimized supply chain is greatly decreased.

As your customers formulate their enterprise supply chain, business system plans, assessing cost and feasibility your opportunity to collaborate is tremendous.

Your customer needs to ensure their plan is aligned with and supports the strategic goals of their overall business. Your goal is to support wherever they require your supply chain services.

As a 3PL sales executive you must have a strong relationship with your customers in order to collaborate at this level. This means getting involved even in strategic decisions early, before final decisions are made.

Strategies and complexities for supply chains increase as we evaluate 3PL's, NVOCC's, truckers, courier companies and their need to collaborate to provide visibility. In this aspect we are talking about both asset and non asset based 3PL's.

The complexity of imports and export processes along with a variety of different country rules and government regulations will further complicate the visibility of the supply chain.

The endeavor becomes more complex as we continue to look deeper into the supply chain.

- **Will your customer extend a fuller visibility and collaboration effort to larger customers and use the old 80/20 rule and involve key accounts and key suppliers only?**

- **Is the cost to integrate prohibitive or are there other solutions that can be utilized?**

The trend in supply chains are towards more complexity since trading under the "globalization" where cross border sourcing is more and more common.

Collaboration for selected parts of the supply chain may be the only option with less collaboration for low value providers. Increasingly global operations will require global coordination, planning and collaboration which in this case renders the systems approach fundamentally more important.

Your customer will look at supply chain requirements aligning purchasing, manufacturing, operations, marketing, sales, finance, inventory and fulfillment. This overall end to end process becomes a necessity in order to create a sustainable solution.

Certain steps in sales and demand forecasts must be clearly coordinated with production plans and many processes need to be standardized. There is a need to actively monitor all aspects in the supply chain to quickly being able to adapt and evolve as needs, changes and challenges arise.

- The overall goal will be to ensure that the company is managing to the same set of financial measures, sales and business goals.

As a 3PL executive you need to understand the customers complete supply chain to effectively inject where you can provide services.

The real issue here is of course which system or combination of systems can provide supply chain visibility?

- System requirements are obviously not the same for all companies. I will only make an attempt to high light some of the most common systems that are used in supply chain visibility.

Many factors will also restrict companies from using certain systems, such as cost, IT resources, time to implement, ROI, other systems priorities, legacy systems, lack of opportunity to collaborate with vendors and suppliers.

Many 3PL's have created their own systems to supplement and make available to customers via a web interface. Some of the data feeds may even come from the systems I mention below. A certain part of these 3PL systems can also be manual input from shipping documents to enhance any aspect that has not been designed with automated data retrieval process.

The typical systems that are involved in many of the supply chain transactions are independent in some respects and collaborative in others. Most systems have a web process and for this reason and can be accessed by many across the globe. Many of these software solutions are also available as a SaaS (Software as a Service) or sometimes referred to as "on demand software". Several of these products are also hosted in the "cloud" and it can at times make these solutions more viable and affordable.

Some of those systems are;

APS – Advanced Planning Systems

WMS – Warehouse Management Systems

ERP – Enterprise Resource Planning system

MRP - Material Requirements Planning

DRP – Demand Replenishment Planning

TMS – Transportation Management Systems, Shipping Systems

YMS – Yard Management Systems

OMS – Order Management Systems

CRM – Customer Relationship Management systems

Within these systems there are numerous processes that make the supply chain operations function.

Some typical processes are

- **Inventory optimization**

- **Replenishment**

- **Fulfillment**

- **VMI (Vendor Manage Inventory), JIT (Just In Time)**

- **Order management**

- **Reverse logistics**

- **Procurement**

- **Purchasing**

- **Planning and forecasting**

- **Network optimization**

- **Materials management**

- **Quality management**

- **ATP (Available To Promise) process**

- **Life cycle management**

- **Labor management**

- **Invoicing**

- **Hub management**

All of these systems have extensive reporting capabilities which will provide data between systems. Adding a data warehouse to these systems can be an good additional solution.

APS is probably one of the most versatile types of systems that can create a supply chain visibility from end to end. It interconnects with many processes and has the ability to view the material and processes throughout the global supply chain. Many large multinational corporations use this kind of software.

WMS has evolved and what used to be a strict warehouse process system is now expanded beyond the four walls . It gives insight into many areas and can provide supply chain visibility throughout the total supply chain.

There are different levels of WMS systems and they are classified as Tier 1 and Tier 2. The first Tier is obviously the more elaborate system and also more expensive. Most of these specific supply chain processes are accessible by web applications.

Some of the solutions within a WMS relates to Multi-Channel Order Management, Global Inventory Visibility, Supply Chain event and synchronization. Like the APS some of the WMS can also order from anywhere and fulfill from any location. This is a business model with a comprehensive "promise to order" against inventory anywhere.

The transportation end of the supply chain would then be used to fulfill the order and optimize the transportation expense.

TMS is sometimes interwoven with the ERP or WMS but can also stand alone.

These systems are execution or transactional systems but are a critical part of the transportation optimization. These systems are available as in house-license, hosted (remote or SaaS). The TMS is used both for inbound and outbound procurement and shipping. A TMS module will typically suggest various shipping solutions and provides information to be evaluated for best option. The TMS can generate the electronic order to engage the transportation with track and trace. It will link back to ERP and WMS to provide the data and update other software modules. This can be used for audit and payment settlement as well.

I elected to make a special mention of Shipping Systems, since they mostly deal with parcel shipping and not with FTL and LTL. The Shipping System is designed to also function as an execution system and will provide optimization for rate, route, label production and all relevant shipping data for parcel shipping. Many of these systems can be customized to handle ecommerce and rate shop like a TMS between the courier companies based on characteristics, delivery date and destination zip code.

The above is a short explanation of some of the turn key supply chain systems. I urge you to further study the systems you are not familiar with and add more details to better comprehend the different variables in a complex global supply chain.

- If your supply chain looks like this, please take every step to correct it.

Virtual logistics

In order to be able to sell and collaborate under the "SCM Principle" your company should be either a true global logistics provider or have the virtual logistics alliances required to support a total handling of the different functions within a complete supply chain. Your company may also be one of the important components of this chain and provide an essential service to other logistics providers. Regardless of whether you are an ocean freight carrier or a trucker, these virtual alliances will be one of the most important aspects (if it isn't already) to survive total global expansion of the supply chains.

These alliances and partnerships will have to be considered for all modes of logistics suppliers. They have to be considered for domestic coverage, as well as, foreign markets. Some partnerships will have to include cultural alliances to ensure that you can provide "total" coverage and delivery of cargo in any market including a foreign market. Many 3PL's, OTI/NVOCC's or ocean carriers have traditionally concentrated on the typical to and from "home or base" market and may still elect to be a "niche" player. In reality a growing segment is actually Corporations buying from or manufacturing in a foreign market and shipping directly to another foreign market thus bypassing the home market completely. This places more emphasis on the sales executive to understand the total supply chain. It becomes evident that sophisticated training is required since the decision makers for many of these foreign to foreign shipping is actually located in your own country.

KPI – Key Performance Indicators

I have talked about how to differentiate yourselves from your competition and of course there are many ways to do so both from an infrastructure point of view as well as systems and operations.

As a red line through all of these types of opportunities runs the KPI's (Key Performance Indicators) that a customer can or should be asking for.

Should you not be using this to your advantage and start talking your customers' language and become a closer partner to your customer then you have been?

Indicating and demonstrating that you are willing to undertake collaboration and <u>measure</u> yourself is one very important step.

Many of us already measure and report on performance on a regular basis, but how many actually sit down with the customer and ask specific questions and define their requirements or industry requirements as to what should be measured?

The parcel carriers, UPS, FedEx, DHL and USPS can be measured and the one KPI they all "deliver" on is on time delivery. For them a high score on a continuous basis is simply certification for survival. This KPI confirms that they are doing a great job that keeps the end customer satisfied.

So are we as proactive as we should be in the supply chain industry as a 3PL, 4PL, Global Freight forwarder, Steam ship Line, air carrier, trucker, courier and all of us in related functions?

Let's evaluate some suggestions on what to measure that would make some sense within the supply chain or logistics functions.

Please keep in mind that KPI's are often specific to an industry or specific customer requirements.

In order to define required KPI's you need to focus on what is important to your customer and what they are having challenges with.

You can also suggest what you are currently measuring as a standard. Don't forget to keep in mind that you are looking for that specific improvement statement from your customer, the one that will make the customer more dependent on you. The KPI's that your customer really wants is the key to keeping the customer.

Some of the areas to be measured could be within;

1. **On-time delivery**, here you can offer measurement in every segment that is under your control and offer suggestions for the areas that you do not handle.
2. **Dock-to-dock ratio** will be a true and quick measurement regardless if this is from the dock in China or the dock in California to destination.
3. **Inventory turn-over/inventory turns** is maybe not critical to you on the onset, but if you are handling the distribution this becomes a real and important measure.
4. **Logistic cost/unit**, just by breaking down the cost and measure the moving components will give you insight as to areas of improvement and processes that may be causing delays. It may even be best to evaluate pure transportation cost per delivery segment.

5. **Delivery performance** of vendors, this could be the local vendors or it can be your supplier's vendors if you are looking deeper into the supply chain

6. **Obsolete and slow moving inventory**, here you can be proactive and flag inventory for your customer that is not moving or have sufficient turns. Maybe move to another type of facility to reduce storage costs?

7. **Shortages**, product or partial delivery of a shipment or out of stock issues.

8. **Reduction in lead time**, domestic and international.

9. **Damages** – ratio per segment in the supply chain
   a. Can packaging be improved?
   b. Engineering services (?)

10. **Vendor measurements**
    a. Ask if you can assist and to what level
    b. If you can, maybe offer a PO management process

11. **Inventory accuracy**
    a. DC labor cost per unit, put away, receiving, shipping
    b. Miss picks per a certain number of lines that makes sense

12. **System performance**
    a. Your system reliability, connectivity, down time
    b. Reports design, data selection – how to improve

13. **Cost to change.** This is somewhat difficult to get into but needs to be addressed in any area of KPI or when you recognize a change is required. Any continuous improvement project would fall under this area to be justifiable. Even small changes can cost a lot in both capital and allocated time. Many companies have "ripple effects" that we as supply chain providers may not be made aware of. For this reason it may be imperative to communicate any change throughout an entire company. You have to make certain that the change being considered does not interrupt any other company process and cause an overall negative effect.

The Supply Chain Council has also developed the SCOR (Supply Chain Operations Reference) model. This is a tool that can be used for many applications as well and worth considering.

The key to doing this right lies in a good and sensible balance of KPI's and not to over do this aspect.

You are looking for opportunities to improve so be cognizant of the right amount of KPI's.

The steps that may follow KPI processes could be in the area of continuous improvement. Depending on what area you decide to address there are several Lean tools for process improvement. Some of the most common include Six Sigma, Kaizen, Value Stream Mapping, 5S and A3.

C-TPAT – Customs Trade Partnership Against Terrorism

Security is becoming a more important part of our Supply Chains and I wanted to bring this into focus as well.

The **Customs-Trade Partnership Against Terrorism** (C-TPAT) is a voluntary supply chain program led by U.S. Customs and Border Protection (CBP) and focused on improving the security of private companies supply chains with respect to terrorism. The program was launched in November 2001 with seven initial participants, all large U.S. companies.

This should be part of your sales discussion to either suggest to your customer that they should participate in this or to verify that they are already part of this. I recognize that many of the 3PL's, Supply Chain providers are already certified and this is a value add that assists the customer. Regardless it should still be evaluated if the customer could benefit by becoming certified themselves.

The threats surrounding the supply chains are growing and becoming more complex with globalization. The supply chain risks at all levels and all aspect must be evaluated. Any security incidents can cause significant disruption to your supply chains and the impact can be financially and otherwise very costly for both your customer and you.

Global Sales Executive

The characteristics and definition of a global sales executive is in many respects in line with the requirements outlined in the section for a Global and National account sales. A greater emphasis has to be placed on a more significant knowledge of a variety of foreign markets.

This kind of experience is typically obtained from someone who already has international sales knowledge and has traveled extensively. Common sense dictates that you should always make certain to understand some of the basic "rules" and customs when you are selling in a foreign environment. As an example a simple point such as several European countries like Germany uses the last name as a normal way of conducting business. Once you have confirmed a first name basis with a German customer you have really achieved a higher level of trust as well as a certain degree of a personal relationship. In other countries such as in Scandinavia a first name is virtually the only accepted way of addressing anyone.

There is a dissimilarity in mentality between many European countries and even though their geographic proximity is close to each other, just crossing over that border to the next country is a world of difference. To be truly successful when selling abroad whether you are in Asia, Europe or the Middle East you must take the time to study their environment and their cultures.

Commonly it is not enough to just study these scenarios, you can only understand the sometimes subtle difference by living in those countries. However, study this aspect is important since your effort will be noticed and could still make the difference in making a sale.

I consider this type of sales executive with this kind of background and experience as part of the "elite" in sales.

This type of selected sales executives brings to mind a past experience regarding a man I met while walking on the beach one afternoon in Miami. He was wearing a white T-shirt with a lot of text on it.

It intrigued me since usually any message on a T-shirt is short to get your attention and enable you to read it quickly. Since he was walking a little bit ahead of me and slower I quickly increased my speed (exercise is still good for me), and when I was within reading distance I slowed my pace (to catch my breath...I need more exercise) to be able to read. It said;

THERE IS NOT TOO MANY OF THE VERY BEST OF US AROUND

I think that this statement says it all about a top notch global sales executive.

MY BEST ADVICE

LISTEN !!!!!

Concentration can only be said to be satisfactory when we can apply it at any moment of our lives to whatever subject or problem we desire.

-D.H. Laurence

Applying and allocating your time is difficult and please remember this; Nobody can manage time, but you can manage those things that take up time.

In order to listen you actually have to SHUT UP!!

- Listen is easy as long as you can be quiet long enough.

- Don't think you have the answer before you have heard them out.

- As hard as it may be, don't talk until the person you are talking to is finished, this is part of being able to shut up and listen.

- **Success will follow after this...**

GLOSSARY OF USEFUL TERMS AND ABBREVIATIONS

ATA Carnet

Document for temporary customs clearance, no duty or VAT is to be paid. An ATA Carnet can be designed to transport and customs clear one product for a for a multitude of countries. This is a special document obtained at selected Chambers of Commerce or Insurance companies. In the USA The United States Council for International Business is the sole issuer and guarantor.

ATA

Actual Time of Arrival

BAF

Bunker Adjustment Factor. Freight adjustment to reflect current cost of bunker/fuel.

B/L

Bill of Lading. Official transportation document. Acts as receipt of goods and contains the terms and conditions of carriage. Also functions as the document that dictates title of goods.

BONDED STORAGE

Designated storage of merchandise under a customs act permitting storage without the payment of duties and taxes.

BOX

Popular name for a container.

BREAK-BULK CARGO

Goods shipped loose in the ships cargo hold.

CABAF

A combination of CAF and BAF.

CAF

Currency adjustment factor to allow for currency fluctuations. This factor have variables from 5 - over 30%.

Certificate of Insurance

Document presented by the insurance company or insured as evidence that insurance is in effect. The insured may assign their rights under this negotiable document to a third party, usually the consignee, by endorsing the reverse of the certificate.

C&F

Cost and Freight. A conventional port to port INCOTERM of sales.

CFS

Container Freight Station. Facility for loading and unloading of LCL cargo.

CFR

Cost and Freight. A conventional port to port INCOTERM of sales.

CIF

Cost Insurance and Freight. A conventional port to port INCOTERM of sales.

CPT

Carriage Paid To. An INCOTERM commonly used when combined modes of transports are utilized.

CROSS DOCKING

Term used where product is received in a warehouse, usually in carload or truck load quantity, for sortation, beyond shipping, or local delivery. Merchandise by-passes the storage function. Documentation in advance of merchandise arrival, or with the shipment itself, will provide name of the ultimate consignee, address, number of pieces and weight. Product should be pre-addressed for final delivery.

CSC

Container Service Charge. A fee levied in conjunction with transit of container through port.

CY

Container Yard. Holding yard for full and empty ocean freight containers. Ocean freight rates are sometimes quoted as CY/CY.

C/O

Certificate of Origin. Document certifying the country of origin issued by a Chamber of Commerce. This document is also commonly legalized by foreign consulates.

CONFERENCE

Organization of a group of ocean freight carriers operating in one trade lane and under the same tariff, rules and regulations.

DDP

Delivered Duty Paid, an INCOTERM term of sales applicable to all modes of transportation.

DEMURRAGE

Charge levied by owner of container/trailer when container is detained longer then the allowable time as outlined in the tariff.

DEPOT

The same as a CFS. Commonly used in certain areas of the world.

DRAWBACK

Repayment of duty after re-exportation of goods. Certain rules must be followed in order to qualify for duty drawback and refund of all duties.

EDI

Electronic Data Interchange. Transfer of data from one computer system to another. Several specific pre-set formats exists for the logistics industry.

ETA

Estimated time of arrival.

ETD

Estimated Time of Departure.

EXW

Ex Works. An INCOTERM term of sales applicable to all modes of transportation.

All charges from Factory are to be brought forward.

FAK

Freight All Kinds. Freight is charged at a certain rate irrespective of actual commodity.

FAS

Free Alongside Ship. A conventional INCOTERM for port to port shipment only.

FCL

Full Container Load.

F.I.F.O.

First In First Out. A warehouse management term. This term indicates that a strict stock rotation is required.

FEU

Forty-foot Equivalent Unit. Popular name for a 40 foot container.

FMC

Federal Maritime Commission. US Federal organization governing ocean freight transportation and rates.

FOB

Free On Board. A conventional INCOTERM for port to port or to point shipment only.

FTL

Full Truck Load.

FTZ

Free Trade Zone. This is a designated area where customs allows goods to be entered without the payment of duties and taxes. Under certain conditions, manipulation or additional transformation of a product is allowed in a FTZ environment. Free Trade Zones exists in most countries.

HONEYCOMBING

A warehouse management term. A condition that results where storage cube potential cannot be utilized because of the great variety and small quantity of each stock keeping unit, i.e. honeycombing.

ISO

International Standards Organization. This organization sets standards and guidelines for operations procedures for a large variety of companies including carriers and forwarders.

Typical certification formats are ISO 9000 and for freight forwarding ISO 9002.

INCOTERMS

International Rules for the Interpretation of Trade Terms.

A set of standard terms for foreign trade contracts. A must have book for any global corporation. These terms outlines the exact obligations for both seller and buyer.

There are a number of less common INCOTERMS that I have not included in this list.

PLEASE SEE INFORMATION BELOW

JIT

Just In Time. Delivery to supply chain or directly to customer upon demand.

LCL

Less Than Container Load. Insufficient volume or weight for a FCL shipment mode. Many LCL shipments are grouped by a carrier or NVOCC to fill a FCL.

Letter of Credit - L/C

Often abbreviated with L/C. The actual bank document stipulating under which terms a particular transaction is undertaken. Method of payment between buyer and seller. The buyer opens a Letter of Credit in favor of the seller at their local bank by depositing the amount of the purchase price and dictating certain documents which the seller must present in order to obtain a payment. Several forms of L/C's exist such as confirmed where payment is guaranteed as long as all terms are met. Another form of L/C is irrevocable which is very common. Sight drafts S/D can be drawn at sight, 30, 60 or any other agreed upon number of days.

L/I

Letter of Indemnity. Can be used to allow a consignee to take delivery of goods without surrendering the B/L. Commonly utilized when documents are late or lost.

L.I.F.O.

Last In First Out. A term indicating a strict stock rotation is not required.

L0-L0

Lift On Lift Off. Movement of containers on and off a vessel by means of lift by crane.

LTL

Less Than Truck load.

MANIFEST

Documents list of goods on a vessel or air craft.

NVOCC

Non Vessel Owning/Operating Common Carrier. A carrier that uses space/containers on a vessel that he neither owns nor operates. Many freight forwarders operate as NVOCC's.

POD

Proof Of Delivery. A signed receipt acknowledging delivery.

RO-RO

A ferry type vessel onto which goods and containers can be driven on and off.

REEFER

Refrigerated. Several containers both air and ocean are popularly called reefers or reefer containers. Refrigerated trucks are also referred to as reefers.

SHORT AND LOW REPORT

Popular warehouse management report. This report states the on hand inventory not allocated for products which have reached a level below a pre-determined minimum position at a specific point of time.

SLIP SHEET

A sheet made of cardboard or plastic used instead of wood or plastic pallet for movement and storage of "pallet" configuration of product.

SOB

Shipped On Board. Endorsement on B/L confirming cargo actually on board a vessel.

SKU

Stock Keeping Unit. Terminology for warehousing of each product in inventory.

STC

Said To Contain. Abbreviation also commonly used as Subject To Count. Used when accepting cargo without physical count.

STEVEDORE

Company which executes the loading, stowing and discharging of vessels.

STRAIGHT BILL OF LADING

This is a non-negotiable B/L.

TEU

Twenty foot Equivalent Unit. Popular name for a twenty foot container.

THC

Terminal Handling Charge. A charge for handling FCL's at ocean freight terminals. Sometimes referred to as Container Service Charge-CSC.

TURNS or TURNOVER

Warehouse management term that states the number of times average inventory is replaced in a given period, usually a month or a year.

ULD

Unit Load Device. Typical name on an air craft container. Several different types of ULD's exists to fit a variety of air crafts.

WMS

Warehouse Management System.

INCOTERMS

Incoterms are incredibly important in trade but please be aware that they also dictate insurance coverage and lines of coverage is often defined by these terms.

Incoterms or **International Commercial terms** are a series of pre-defined commercial terms published by the International Chamber of Commerce (ICC) widely used in international commercial transactions. A series of three-letter trade terms related to common sales practices, Incoterms are intended primarily to clearly communicate the tasks, costs and risks associated with the transportation and delivery of goods. Incoterms are accepted by governments, legal authorities and practitioners worldwide for the interpretation of most commonly used terms in international trade. They are intended to reduce or remove altogether uncertainties arising from different interpretation of such terms in different countries. First published in 1936, Incoterms have been periodically updated, with the eighth version—Incoterms 2010—having been published on January 1, 2011. Incoterms is a registered trademark.

History

Incoterms began development in 1921 with the forming of the idea by the International Chamber of Commerce. In 1936, the first set of Incoterms was published. The first set remained in use for almost 20 years before the second publication in 1953. Additional amendments and expansions followed in 1967, 1976, 1980, 1990 and 2000.

Incoterms 2010

The eighth published set of pre-defined terms, Incoterms 2010 defines 11 rules, reducing the 13 used in Incoterms 2000 by introducing two new rules ("Delivered at Terminal", DAT; "Delivered at Place", DAP) that replace four rules of the prior version ("Delivered at Frontier", DAF; "Delivered Ex Ship", DES; "Delivered Ex Quay", DEQ; "Delivered Duty Unpaid", DDU). In the prior version, the rules were divided into four categories, but the 11 pre-defined terms of Incoterms 2010 are subdivided into two categories based only on method of delivery. The larger group of seven rules applies regardless of the method of transport, with the smaller group of four being applicable only to sales that solely involve transportation over water.

General mode of transportation

The seven rules defined by Incoterms 2010 for general modes of transportation are:

EXW – Ex Works (named place)

The seller makes the goods available at his premises. The buyer is responsible for all charges. This trade term places the greatest responsibility on the buyer and minimum obligations on the seller. The Ex Works term is often used when making an initial quotation for the sale of goods without any costs included. EXW means that a seller has the goods ready for collection at his premises (Works, factory, warehouse, plant) on the date agreed upon. The buyer pays all transportation costs and also bears the risks for bringing the goods to their final destination. The seller delivers the good at seller's premise or named place (works, factory and warehouse, etc), but not loaded on collecting vehicles and not cleared for export. The seller has no obligation to load the goods, even though in practice he may be in a better position to do so. If the seller does load the good, he does so at buyer's risk and cost. If parties wish seller to be responsible for the loading of the goods on departure and to bear the risk and all costs of such loading, this must be made clear by adding explicit wording to this effect in the Contract of sale.

FCA – Free Carrier (named places)

The seller hands over the goods, cleared for export, into the custody of the first carrier (named by the buyer) at the named place. The buyer pays for carriage to the named point of destination, but risk passes when the goods are handed over to the first carrier.

CPT - Carriage Paid to (named place of destination) - Seller pays for main carriage Risk transfers to buyer upon delivery to first carrier rail

CIP – Carriage and Insurance Paid (To) (named place of destination) The containerized transport/multimodal equivalent of CIF. Seller pays for carriage and insurance to the named destination point, but risk passes when the goods are handed over to the first carrier.

DAT – Delivered at Terminal

Seller pays for carriage to the terminal, except for costs related to import clearance, and assumes all risks up to the point that the goods are unloaded at the terminal.

DAP – Delivered at Place (named place of destination)

Seller pays for carriage to the named place, except for costs related to import clearance, and assumes all risks prior to the point that the goods are ready for unloading by the buyer.

DDP – Delivered Duty Paid (destination place)

Seller is responsible for delivering the goods to the named place in the country of importation, including all costs and risks in bringing the goods to import destination. This includes duties, taxes and customs formalities

Water transportation (solely)

The four rules defined by Incoterms 2010 for sales where transportation is entirely conducted by water are:

FAS – Free Alongside Ship (named loading port)

The seller must place the goods alongside the ship at the named port. The seller must clear the goods for export. Suitable only for maritime transport but NOT for multimodal sea transport in containers (see Incoterms 2010, ICC publication 715). This term is typically used for heavy-lift or bulk cargo.

FOB – Free On Board (named loading port)

The seller must themselves load the goods on board the ship nominated by the buyer, cost and risk being divided at ship's rail. The seller must clear the goods for export. Maritime transport only but NOT for multimodal sea transport in containers (see Incoterms 2010, ICC publication 715). The buyer must instruct the seller the details of the vessel and port where the goods are to be loaded, and there is no reference to, or provision for, the use of a carrier or forwarder. It **does not** include Air transport. This term has been greatly misused over the last three decades ever since Incoterms 1980 explained that FCA should be used for container shipments.

CFR – Cost and Freight (named destination port)

Seller must pay the costs and freight to bring the goods to the port of destination. However, risk is transferred to the buyer once the goods are loaded on the ship (this rule is new since 2010!). Maritime transport only and Insurance for the goods is NOT included. Insurance is at the Cost of the Buyer.

CIF – Cost, Insurance and Freight (named destination port)

Exactly the same as CFR except that the seller must in addition procure and pay for insurance for the buyer. Maritime transport only.

Previous terms eliminated in 2010

DAF – Delivered At Frontier (Delivery place)

This term can be used when the goods are transported by rail and road. The seller pays for transportation to the named place of delivery at the frontier. The buyer arranges for customs clearance and pays for transportation from the frontier to his factory. The passing of risk occurs at the frontier.

DES – Delivered Ex Ship (named port)

Where goods are delivered ex ship, the passing of risk does not occur until the ship has arrived at the named port of destination and the goods made available for unloading to the buyer. The seller pays the same freight and insurance costs as he would under a CIF arrangement. Unlike CFR and CIF terms, the seller has agreed to bear not just cost, but also Risk and Title up to the arrival of the vessel at the named port. Costs for unloading the goods and any duties, taxes, etc… are for the Buyer. A commonly used term in shipping bulk commodities, such as coal, grain, dry chemicals - - - and where the seller either owns or has chartered, their own vessel.

DEQ – Delivered Ex Quay (named port)

This is similar to DES, but the passing of risk does not occur until the goods have been unloaded at the port of destination.

DDU – Delivered Duty Unpaid (destination place)

This term means that the seller delivers the goods to the buyer to the named place of destination in the contract of sale. The goods are not cleared for import or unloaded from any form of transport at the place of destination. The buyer is responsible for the costs and risks for the unloading, duty and any subsequent delivery beyond the place of destination. However, if the buyer wishes the seller to bear cost and risks associated with the import clearance, duty, unloading and subsequent delivery beyond the place of destination, then this all needs to be explicitly agreed upon in the contract of sale.

60221878R00144

Made in the USA
Lexington, KY
30 January 2017